The Criminological Mind

The Criminological Mind

Eric Carlton

© Eric Carlton 2010

Published by Shaffron Publishing Ltd

ISBN 978-0-9556155-7-3

Prepared and printed by:

York Publishing Services Ltd
64 Hallfield Road
Layerthorpe
York YO31 7ZQ
Tel: 01904 431213

Website: www.yps-publishing.co.uk

ABOUT THE AUTHOR

Following service with the Parachute Regiment in the UK and overseas, Eric Carlton completed a four-year course in religious studies and then served as a minister in the Midlands and in London. Subsequently he also completed graduate and postgraduate courses in the social sciences at the LSE and the University of Leeds. As an academic he taught for many years at the Universities of Durham and Teesside where he is currently a Research Fellow.

Dr Carlton has written a number of books, some of which are indirectly related to the present volume: Treason, meanings and motives; War and Ideology: Militarism, rule without law; Massacres, an historical perspective: The State against the State, the theory and practice of the coup d'etat.

STRUCTURE

Preface

Introduction: this is a study not of the criminal mind – if, indeed that is knowable – but of the criminological mind, i.e. the ways in which criminologists think about crime and criminality.

It is divided into three sections:

1) theories of criminality

2) a typology of murder (including case studies)

3) Critical and Realist appreciations of crime and punishment

SECTION 1

i) Crime and Criminology – an Overview
Excursus: Crime and Poverty

ii) Classical Theories and Criminology
Moral infirmity and physiological inadequacy

iii) Psychological Theories and Criminology

iv) The Ambiguities of Moral Evasion
Excursus: Are there 'Natural Born Killers' ?

v) Sociological Theories and Criminology
Excursus: Crime and Counselling

PREFACE

There is a tendency – indeed, a propensity – within the social sciences (of which criminology is arguably a sub-genre) to see crime as a social construct. This makes a certain amount of sense as an interpretive exercise, but it is all rather puzzling to the layperson and to many crime professionals (police, judges, etc.). The sorts of questions that are asked by criminologists especially the self-styled 'new criminologists' – are: who decides what is and what is not a crime? who determines its degree of gravity? and especially, how is crime and crime enforcement presented to the public at large?

This is well illustrated in relation to the contentious issue of terrorism. The entire phenomenon appears to be unambiguous in the eyes of the public, but the criminologist wants to know how it is spoken about, written about, photographed and generally portrayed to the public. How is its presentation structured? How are victims depicted? How are the reactions of the authorities portrayed, and how are the declared rationales of the terrorist/ freedom fighter organizations to be interpreted? It is argued that any real understanding of terrorism and terrorists must take into account political, police/security and economic factors. Not least, there is the issue of moral imperatives and society's aesthetic paradigms. In short, crime has multidimensional qualities; it is no one kind of a thing:

There is little doubt that the public will see this as part of a brain-teasing exculpatory exercise. An attempt to excuse or, at least, mitigate what has taken place, possibly by placing the crime in a wider context (e.g. contrasting the act with those of the more horrendous and thus more reprehensible acts of certain multi-national corporations such as those of the tobacco and armaments industries in the Third World), or by seeking mitigating circumstances in the backgrounds of the criminals themselves.

Whilst not minimizing the extent of high-level white-collar crime (indeed, the highly questionable activities of governments which either tend to get overlooked or are not seen as 'crimes', as such) there is surely no serious dispute as to the *objective* nature of most actual crime. A murder is a murder, it is the taking of a life (or lives), even if the degree of culpability has to be assessed and punishment judged accordingly.

While appreciating 'new criminology' perspectives which tend to be as concerned with judicial and enforcement procedures as about epistemological issues, this text is, by and large, prepared to accept general social definitions of crime. Furthermore, it supports – with certain common-sense reservations – the roles of the police and the courts despite their inconsistencies and possible injusticies. It does not see any really viable alternative to some form of prison system, and takes the view that – if anything – the courts are too lenient on certain types of crime (e.g. drugs offences). Furthermore, it endorses the view – no longer popular among 'progressives' – that punishment should not only be reformative but also retributive. Society has the right to punish those who flout its rules, and a duty to protect itself from – hopefully further infractions of its legal codes.

SECTION 1

Theories of Criminality

i) CRIME AND CRIMINOLOGY: AN OVERVIEW

It should be noted from the outset that this is not a book about *the criminal mind*. Indeed, if such a thing exists it is almost certainly unknowable. There is undoubtedly what we might term criminal mindedness, a tendency or inclination to act in a criminal way, but this will be related to the crime(s) in question. Similarly with the term deviant. Most of us are deviant in some way or another, and have probably committed acts which may or may not be categorized as deviant depending on who is doing the categorizing and how the term is to be defined.

On the other hand, it is possible to talk about the criminological mind, the ways in which criminologists think about crime and the kinds of theories they adduce to try to account for criminal acts. These theories, which some may regard as more and others less than convincing, fall into a few commonly accepted categories: absolutist (moral) theories, physiological theories which concentrate on the brain's mechanisms, psychological theories centered on the proclivities of the individual (at which point the criminological mind would appear to shade into the criminal mind), and sociological theories which stress the importance of social factors relating to crime. None of these is totally persuasive, and none gives any more than a plausible explanation. Indeed, taken together they cannot – and should never claim – to explain everything. But insofar as they can shed some light on the subject they can be useful. In time, no doubt, they will be refined, but inadequate as they. may be, at the moment they are all we have.

As far as we can tell there has always been an interest in the nature and causes of crime. In very early law-codes such as the famous inscribed prescriptions on the stele of Hammurabi who ruled in Mesopotamia c1750 B.C., the king's advisers were keen on detail, even to the point of prescribing how a builder was to be punished if his house collapsed on the occupants. On the other hand, in the ancient world's companion society, Egypt, we are told that,'law emanates from the mouth of the Pharaoh'. This suggests a kind of arbitrariness in Egyptian law, whereas, as far as we can make out, it was largely based on precedent – not unlike much English law, both civil and criminal. There have, of course, been innumerable law codes since, not least those of the Romans who are as famous for their laws as for their roads. They were not the greatest exemplars for posterity, but their ideas were such that Napoleon saw fit to incorporate many of them into his own law-code. English law too has strong Roman associations. However, criminology is only indirectly connected with law codes in that it is much more concerned with patterns of crime as well as the 'predisposing factors' – if indeed they can be discerned – which cause individuals and groups to act in a criminal way.

Criminology then – though not by that name – has been with us since people were concerned about the infraction of the rules. Today it is considered to be an important sub-discipline which incorporates elements of generally recognized disciplines such as sociology (particularly in its introduction of deviance theory), psychology, history, law, and more marginally, economics (although the issue of crime and property relations is by no means unimportant). These disciplines have been influential, and have made the main theoretical contributions to criminology, although it should be emphasized that despite alternative claims, so far no one overall or satisfactory theory or set of theories has been forthcoming.

The first section of the book is a critical examination of these theories, and an attempt to evaluate their varying degrees of plausibility. The second section is devoted to an analysis of just one form of crime – the taking of life, which may be classified as murder or manslaughter (a term that is ever more liberally interpreted). The third section rounds off the discussion with some consideration of the problem of culpability and the vexed question of punishment and retribution.

In the simplest terms, crime is said incontrovertibly to be the infraction of the criminal law. But for many – perhaps most – criminologists crime is whatever a society decides is crime. Such a definition has an unsatisfactory circularity and does not explain *why* a crime *is* a crime, nor does it delineate the criteria upon which such a judgement is made, except perhaps to make highly generalized references to the violation of individual autonomy and the dangers to the fabric of society. Indeed, we will find that the more radical criminologists are not at all happy with generalized statements concerning social precedents, and prefer to 'negotiate' particular situations as and when they arise.

This more radical view, particularly associated with sociologists such as Jock Young (1980) and Stanley Cohen (1980) seems particularly relevant where new laws have to be made (for example, in relation to the misuse of drugs) or where a shift or important change in the law is either made or proposed. A very obvious case in point would be the issue of homosexual law reform. Homosexuality among males was a criminal act in the UK until 1969 (interestingly homosexual acts among women seems hardly to have been recognized). This followed from the-Wolfenden Report (1967) which while still condemning overt homosexual acts, effectively decriminalized private acts among consenting adults (adult being another term which has been redefined). This change took. place not just because the lawmakers felt that they could take a more lenient view of homosexual relations, but also because it was felt that some changes ought to be made regarding the regulation or otherwise of private conduct.

It should be noted, however, that this says nothing about the nature or quality of the acts concerned; this is a moral question which should also be considered. Neither does it properly take into account the fact that where extreme violence is used and participants regard themselves as having been abused, the relevant law can be invoked. (A similar situation can arise where 'rough-trade' heterosexual activity can turn into an unwanted form of rape).

It really goes without saying then that definitions of crime have changed over the years. For instance, the recent discovery of a Chinese vessel which sank off the coast of Indonesia in 1822 with a luxurious cargo of porcelain and the loss of 1800 lives was a reminder of a more insidious but quasi-legal and lucrative trade. Some survivors were rescued by a British ship which was carrying opium into China in such quantities that it was wreaking havoc on the population and,the economy.

Perceptions of culpability have also changed over time. We all know that in Britain in the late 18th century children as young as seven could be hanged for stealing goods worth only a few pennies, presumably on the assumption that if they were allowed to live they would only be a greater menace to society. It may surprise some to know that at about the same time there were actually over a hundred offences punishable by death including impersonating a Chelsea Pensioner and defacing Waterloo Bridge.

There seems to be a perennial debate about whether crime is or is not on the increase. This, of course, has to depend upon which periods are being compared, and pre-eminently of which kinds of crime are involved. Crime can be analysed in terms of a number of different variables; area/location, type of crime, age, sex and class of the victim, resolution rate and so forth, but there are so many things that police and court statistics don't tell us. Official statistics do allow for certain comparisons to be made, but there is always the criticism that they may reflect personal or institutional biases, or may indicate ongoing social concerns (sometimes referred to as 'moral panics') such as paedophilia which come to special public attention periodically.

There is also the additional reservation that official statistics tell us little or nothing about 'hidden crime' such as indecent assault, date rape and domestic violence which for various reasons may go unreported. One possible reason for this is that unlike reporting, say, a theft, no kind of restitution is possible (a stolen bicycle may be returned or insurance may be claimed, but this is hardly possible with a person's dignity and self-respect). There is also what is misleadingly termed 'victimless crime'. This refers to crimes such as fraud where trust and probity have been violated within the business community. Yet there are still victims, shareholders for instance, even if the losses are widely distributed. Indeed it is arguable whether any crime is entirely 'victimless'. A subtle example would be that of the taking of illicit drugs to enhance performance in high level sports. The Olympic gold medallist Florence 'Flo-Jo' Joyner 'who held world records at 100 and 200 metres, almost certainly won her later races with the aid of drugs. This is now generally accepted. There seems to have been' no other way in which the sudden increase in her musculature and performance can be accounted for. It may even be that the ingestion of high doses of HGH (Human Growth Hormone) also contributed to her early death at 38 in September 1998. The victims were her fellow competitors.

Furthermore, crime statistics often reveal very little, if anything, about certain high-level forms of white collar crime whether it is corporate/economic crime which can range from insider dealing to industrial espionage, or political crime which often involves such offences as perjury and illegal payments. One wonders if there is that much difference in principle between cash-far-questions in the British

Parliament over which there has been a considerable furore, and the money-raising junkets often arranged by political parties at which paying guests. can ask privileged questions of the highly-placed hosts. The Tory, William Hague, for example, has held such 'forums' where wealthy businessmen are invited if they can guarantee a minimum of £10,000 for the Party – a practice which is certainly not confined to British Conservatives. It is just one of a number of strategems adopted to enhance Party coffers. The Tory Front Bench club markets itself as a group of loyal supporters at £5,000 a time. It arranges functions at which members can meet shadow cabinet ministers. The Labour Party, on the other hand, has a 1000 Club where donors pay a £1000 a year – and this is not to mention the honours given to notables who have contributed generously to the 'private office'.

And official statistics certainly don't tell us much about the nature and extent of organized crime about which the public only becomes aware when a sensational case hits the headlines such as the relatively recent drugs-related murder of three men found in a Landrover in Essex. The term organized crime is normally used where there is a hierarchical structure of individuals engaged in an ongoing pattern of criminal activity such as prostitution, drugs, and so forth. Organized or syndicate crime often involves corruption and intimidation of the agencies of law enforcement, and in some instances may be associated with so-called secret societies of one kind or another such as the Tongs, the Mafia, the Cosa Nostra, and – in a qualified sense – the Loyalist and Republican 'paramilitary groups in Northern Ireland who needed continually to replenish their treasuries.

In terms of scale, the prize probably goes to white collar crime and its 'poorer' counterpart blue collar crime. The term 'white collar crime' originated with the work of Edwin Sutherland (1949) whose earlier studies had been concerned with the professional thief (1937). The term is self-explanatory and refers to crimes such as tax frauds, embezzlement, and illegal wheeling and dealing of various kinds. Often we associate this type of crime with the affluent such as the Guinness affair a few years ago which was particularly notable for the miraculous way in which one of the principals who claimed to be suffering from dementia made an astonishingly rapid recovery, and thus avoided punishment. White collar crime is therefore in a special sense professional crime and may not always be immediately apparent. Unless all the necessary safeguards are in place it may be difficult to detect, especially in the short term. And there is some evidence to suggest that it is sometimes treated with more tolerance than it deserves. Admittedly, it doesn't involve violence, but where, say, a company or possibly a bank collapses having effectively defrauded its share holders or depositors, the result can be devastating for those concerned. And it is made that much more difficult to bear when it is discovered that their money has been used to support the extravagant lifestyle of one or more of its directors. One authority, (Giddens 1991) quoting a US study states that it is estimated that white collar crime (mainly involving fraud of one kind and another) probably nets forty times as much as crimes against property (car theft, burglaries and the like).

Blue collar crime is what we might otherwise call petty crime, but as recent studies have shown it is by no means inconsequential. Employee theft, for example, is one of the most prevalent and costly – and often hidden – problems confronting modern businesses, and by its nature doesn't show up in the crime statistics. It is sometimes 'neutralized' by' misleading or euphemistic terminology such as 'fiddling', 'shrinkage' or 'non-violent property deviance'. But repeated minor incidences add up over time to such an extent that it is now estimated that in the UK it is ten times more costly than street crime (including shop-lifting), and accounts for over a third of business failures (Business File Sunday Telegraph 17 September 2000). It is obvious that many people are quite conscience less about taking illicitly from organizations, although they would be very hesitant about stealing from private individuals.

(Typically in 'total organizations' such as the military, pilfering from the stores or the cookhouse is seen as fair game, but stealing from 'mates' is a heinous offence). Complementarily, firms are often reluctant to prosecute employees, possibly because they do not regard the offence as really criminal. Instead they may invoke some form of in-house sanction such as deductions of salary. This hushes the whole thing up, and helps to preserve the right image as well as saving legal expenses.

Another related category is what is sometimes termed 'social crime'. This would normally include such offences as trespassing, poaching, wood theft and rioting – acts which are said with some justification to have been criminalized by the ruling class. Also within this general category we could probably include smuggling – an offence which in the UK has shades of Dr. Syn, and was once associated with the Cornish coast 200 years ago when smugglers were proscribed along with highwaymen. But with the high taxes on certain goods today, smuggling has once more become a lucrative activity both for the professional (narcotics) and the amateur (tobacco and alcohol).

Changes in public and legal attitudes towards crime raises the vexed issue of decriminalization. And in no area of activity is this more talked about than in the debate about drugs. It hardly needs stressing that every society has rules which imply some kind of majority agreement. These may be *imposed rules* which are considered to be mandatory such as legal restrictions, or they may be *implied rules* of an informal kind such as being truthful, fair and so forth. Every society has to have codes of some kind, and most also have an authority to enforce these codes where necessary. But what happens when there is a groundswell of opinion for a change in the rules, or where there is a powerful or vociferous lobby agitating for change? How, as with the drugs issue, can changes toward leniency be made (because that is what agitation is usually about), and at the same time ensure that there will not be the abuses that more orthodox opinion fears?

Those who have advocated the reclassification of certain drugs, particularly cannabis, argue that it would make the drug openly available and thus reduce the criminal element from the market. For example in Marshall (1998) we find the view that 'The concept of addiction is unhelpful; it suggests a dependency with grave consequences for the individual and for society. Not all drug users develop dependency nor do such consequences inevitably follow; the term problem drug user is therefore increasingly favoured. Regarding crime, the dominant thesis is that regular drug use, coupled with the illegality of supply, forces users to commit crime in order to pay for drugs; however, whether drug use leads to involvement in crime or involvement in delinquent life-styles introduces a person to drug use, is debated....(but) calls for decriminalization are regularly made'.

The counter argument is that if this were done there is no guarantee that users would not graduate to harder drugs such as heroin and cocaine, and that anyway some research indicates that cannabis may be harmful in itself. Quite apart from the medical pros and cons, the whole decriminalization debate implies that in order to reduce crime all we have to do is to take particular crimes off the statute book (its a little like saying that if we want to obviate the agonies of divorce all we need to do is to do away with marriage). All we can say at this stage is that the social experiments in decriminalization in Holland and Switzerland have not been notably successful and that they now appear to be reconsidering their policies.. Relaxation of the law may not therefore be the answer (Carlton 1995).

From what we have seen in this brief overview it seems to be very clear that crime statistics are not entirely reliable for a number of reasons. They are based on lots of notifiable recorded offences, on police statistics and criminological research and it is known that these may be subject to bias. But it is well known that there is both unreported and underreported crime, perhaps because it will entail some embarrassment or because, for one reason or another, it will be an unproductive procedure. Sociologists in particular have been quick to point out that much depends upon how society chooses to define criminal behaviour, and this – as we have seen – may change over time or with respective jurisdictions (in the UK, the recent decisions on devolution are bound to lead to problems of comparison, as does the issue of state and federal offences in the USA). However, this is not to suggest – as some ethnostatisticians – that crime figures cannot in any sense be taken as objective indications of what actually takes place since they are subject to human interpretation and distortion or, as some ethnomethodologists, that the production of statistics is itself the 'real' topic of investigation.

One thing we haven't touched on and concerning which the question of 'official statistics' is irrelevant is international crime such as terrorism and conspiracy. Or when a state uses its monopoly of force in what the international community regards as a criminal way. This would include the waging of aggressive war in order to further socio-economic ends, or for some ideological objective, which mayor may not entail atrocity and massacre. This may well be categorized as the very worst form of crime, if only because it is carried' out on such a large scale. It will therefore merit some treatment in Section 11, although, strictly speaking, it is outside the normal purview of criminalologists.

EXCURSUS: CRIME AND POVERTY

The issue of social background is considered critical to much criminological debate. Especially germane, from the point of view of many investigators is the question of deprivation. But much depends on how this term is defined. The more sociologically sophisticated prefer the term 'relative deprivation', an expression which initially seems to be more acceptable, except that there is a sense in which we are all deprived relative to something or someone, whether socially, economically, physically, intellectually or whatever.

However, if we take the term at face value – which really means that we do not press the matter of alternative meanings too hard – there is a positive correlation between poverty and certain forms of crime, though we must be careful here to distinguish between correlation and causation. There may well be a certain kind of relationship between these two variables but this does not mean that we can always trace or explain exactly what constitutes the nature of that relationship. We may find, for instance, that crime – even a career of crime – may not result primarily from economic deprivation (i.e. poverty) as much as status deprivation, i.e. being well thought of by a particular social milieu, as was the case with the East End's Kray brothers.

If we look for example, at a report prepared for the Probation Service by researchers at Lancaster University, we find that young offenders by and large fell into the unemployed or unemployable. categories. Of the 1389 offenders aged between '17 and 23, nearly two thirds were unemployed and were on social security benefits, mainly income support. Most had left their parental homes, (one feels constrained to ask why); 26% had, at some time or another, been in local authority care; and about 20% were chronically sick or disabled, including addictions (though obviously not so disabled that they were incapable of committing crimes). The survey showed that even at such a young age 25% had children of their own, although well over half the men were not living with them, and that some 20% had already had a breakdown in their relationships. The sample indicated that there had been considerable disruption in their social circumstances, although we are assured that they had adopted various 'coping strategies' such as loans, use of mail order catalogues and what are euphemistically described as 'survival thefts'.

As far as education was concerned, only 2% had stayed on at school after the minimum leaving age, so the majority (80%) had no formal qualifications at all. About half had attended a government training scheme, although subsequently only half had kept a job for more than six months. Needless to say most respondents had totally negative attitudes towards education, and regarded school knowledge as unrelated to the needs of the real world – a common rationalization rooted in the erroneous view that education is simply a way of getting work. Education may enhance job prospects, but essentially it is an end in itself. Sometimes respondents blamed themselves for their unenviable predicament, but they were also quick to cite such incommensurables as stress, pressure, disruption etc., categories that one suspects were conveniently provided by researchers in their questionnaires.

This survey which was conducted by the use of questionnaires supplemented by interviews is now somewhat dated, although the overall situation has not changed *that* much. This can be seen from a more recent study carried out under the auspices of the Child Poverty Action Group. The tone of this study is set in the Foreword by human rights advocate and QC Michael Mansfield who maintains that we live in a society which entertains 'the vilification of the vulnerable: immigrants, lone mothers, homeless people and the unemployed (who are regarded as) uncomfortable, inconvenient, unsightly, unnecessary.... a burden within a culture of dependency'. This is endorsed early in the main text by a quotation from an anonymous police constable who avers that 'society cannot blame the poor for their crimes if it offers them no hope for the future and tolerates gross inequalities of income and wealth' (Cook, 1997, p.3). Cook makes it clear from the beginning that she in no way approves of the 'Victorian idea' of the 'dishonest or undeserving poor' a segment of society who are noted for the social irresponsibility and personal fecklessness. This is seen as an outdated concept. Indeed, the whole idea of dealing with social ills by some kind of remoralization of society is repudiated. The remedy should not start with the individual – as remoralization implies – but with the reorganization of society and an equalization of citizens' life chances.

The present text argues that poverty should be seen as a *source* rather than a *cause* of crime. This is a fine distinction which really requires some elaboration. We do not need to be told that poverty does not inevitably lead to crime, a fact well illustrated by the lack of crime amidst acute poverty in the Welsh valleys between the wars.

Indeed, this only serves to support the traditional contention that there is *less* reason to listen so assiduously to those who excuse crime on the grounds of poverty. Again we should perhaps think of *some* crime as the indirect result of social exclusion. This is often related to the perception of elites who appear to prosper without too much productivity (yet paradoxically admire the denizens of the pop culture who prosper without too much talent). Furthermore, crimes which are not committed for any obvious economic gain such as vandalism, "joy-riding", drug abuse, and certain forms of domestic violence, cannot easily be explained in terms of unemployment and poverty.

Prostitution and Social Security fraud are likewise seen by some as crimes of poverty, but this too surely needs serious qualification. It is true that they often represent disorganized rather than organized crime, but it is surely fallacious to suppose that they are the last or only economic resort of the majority of those involved. Surely in most cases there is an alternative of some kind; after all, some of the younger members of the horizontally challenged community still hope to make it into the big-time. This is not, however, to suggest that when prostitutes themselves become victims of crime, they in some sense deserve what they get. Prostitution, especially at the seamier levels can be a hazardous profession, catering as it often does for those with deviant and rather bizarre tastes. But it is unjust for society to regard them as deserving victims of sometimes outrageous abuse.

The problem with writers such as Cook et al, is the very marked tendency to see crime as something that derives almost exclusively from social circumstances rather than from the individual psyche. The bias can be seen in such statements as, 'irrespective of whether they actually commit crime, the poverty stigma and targeting of these groups makes it more likely that their behaviour will be policed and criminalized' – a sentiment that smacks ominously of conspiracy theory. It should always be remembered that much crime is by disadvantaged people against other disadvantaged people. Of course, poor social conditions are very important, and can be convincingly correlated with the incidence of crime. But the prevalence of white collar, high profile crime should warn us that poverty and crime are not inextricably associated. Certainly we should beware of making unwarranted causal connections between poverty and crime, and complementarily to be wary of looking upon offenders as the 'true' victims of society. Those of us who grew up with the maxim that 'trifles make perfection' will therefore be more sympathetic to the practice of zero tolerance than those who seek exculpatory reasons for criminal and anti-social behaviour.

ii) CLASSICAL THEORIES AND CRIMINOLOGY

Classical theories are sometimes termed absolutist theories because they imply a belief in absolute or objective standards whereby human behaviour may be judged. In the 18th century, the classical school in law assumed that humans were rational beings, and were therefore able to exercise free will.

Consequently if all actions were assumed to be willed actions it followed that people were capable of making rational calculations with respect to the costs/benefits/advantages/disadvantages of their actions. The implication for criminal policy was 'to make the cost of infraction greater than the potential benefits' (Jary & Jary,1991, p.130). The idea that crime must not pay, and that the punishment must exceed the crime – if indeed they are commensurable- is basic to modern deterrence policy. Likewise accessible proceeds of criminal activities (such as, for example drug dealing) should be confiscated, because the criminal must not be allowed to profit from his crime.

Such ideas inevitably raise the interesting and much-debated issue as to whether or not humans do actually have free will, or whether in some sense all so-called 'willed' actions are determined. We will consider this question in more detail when we come to look at psychological theories of crime. At the moment it will suffice to consider the moral implications of absolutist ideas which tend to be disparaged by many modern theorists. To put it at its most basic, it is insufficient to argue, as some religious people might, that 'this man committed this crime because he is a sinner'; what one has to ask is why this man committed this particular kind of sin in these particular circumstances? In fact, if our hypothetical critic persisted with this type of argument, it could easily be countered that this form of reasoning is logically circular, and would actually get us nowhere (its rather like saying that people commit crimes because they are criminals).

Yet this is not to undervalue the moral dimensions of crime. Most of us are quite sure that there are such things as right and wrong (as philosopher, Ernest Gellner, once put it in a radio broadcast, 'I believe in objective values, but don't ask me to prove them'). But critics insist that such values are artificial and socially contrived and are constructed simply to ensure the harmonious running of society. What is right in one culture may be seen to be wrong in another. For those who dismiss the idea of objective or fundamental values all so-called criteria for moral behaviour are relative. They change or are modified according to the culture or society in question. Indeed, in practice – so it is argued – behaviour actually changes with the imperatives of the situation. Morality is simply a matter of calculation. People quickly weigh. up the situation and – by and large – do whatever is in their own best interests. (I'm reminded of a New Yorker cartoon in which the tiny figures of a man and a woman are standing on a small plateau in the midst of a mountain range from which there is obviously no easy escape. And the man is saying, 'Let's say that out here, Miss Harrington, that nature makes its own laws').

But a moment's reflection will show us that this initially persuasive idea of moral relativism has its problems. To begin with if all values are relative, what are they relative *to*? Let's take the basic value to preserve human life. Is this relative to states, cultures, groups, individuals, or just particular situations where killing may be justified as in, say, self-defence? The problem is that where everything is relative, nothing can be known to be relative without a fixed point of reference. Without an established bench-mark it is impossible to assess any variations or deviations from the rule. Indeed, these may serve to confirm the validity of the value in question. The fact is that no matter how primitive or historic the culture, we actually find that the perennial values of honesty, truth-telling, reciprocity, bravery and the like are as highly esteemed as they are in modern developed society, even if they are not always strictly observed or expressed in the same way.

The further problem with relativism is that it confuses means with ends. We can see from just a superficial glance at certain diverse forms of human activity ranging from sport to war how this confusion can occur. The *means* of the activity can be varied and relative, but the *ends* – the overall objective – remains much the same. The sorts of things for which humans strive, whether they are primitives or sophisticates, tend to have a great deal in common. Even in the world of organized crime, the same thing obtains. It is known, for example, that many Mafia dons, although both vicious and avaricious, as much as anything are concerned about their good name and that they are given the esteem that they believe they deserve. They together with the equally ruthless Roman emperor, Tiberius, could say, 'I don't care if the people don't love me, as long as they respect me'. It is perhaps not without significance that one authoritative book about the Sicilian Mafia (Catanzaro, 1992) is simply called 'Men of Respect'.

Criminologists may well balk at the idea of moral absolutes, but they have been the abiding concern of philosophers through the ages. Plato, said by some to be the greatest of them all certainly advocated the idea of universal moral values, particularly the ideal of goodness which exists apart from any specific instances or experiences of good acts. And Kant, who brought about something of a revolution in philosophy, though departing somewhat from Plato on the place of reason in human behaviour, argued that if there were no universal categories, and all values were relative, then all meaningful communication between humans would break down. People may dispute the precise application of such values, but if the ground rules are discarded it is difficult to know where to begin.

The notion of moral values inevitably involves the allied notion of ideals, and how these ideals can be reconciled with everyday experience. This raises the question of just how we come to have ideals in the first place. After all, nothing in this life is perfect, yet we still have the conception of perfection of the ideal. Furthermore, in behavioural and intellectual terms some people aspire to the ideal in science, in the professions, in sport, and in their relationships, but usually feel that they never quite succeed. This is true in 'moral matters too. We rarely live up even to our own standards – yet our very failure is a recognition that such standards exist.

The obvious corollary of the moral culpability argument is that as humans we have the freedom to choose how we act. Therefore to choose to commit a criminal act is a function of our moral freedom. But do we actually have freewill? Despite our subjective consciousness that we choose how to act, there is, in fact, no ultimate proof that we possess freewill (I could ask myself why I chose to write the last sentence the way I did, or why I am writing this book at all. Surely, it could be argued, I am doing what I am doing because I *decided* to do it that way? But the determinist would reply that given all possible antecedent factors, I had to do what I did). The 18th century mathematician Pierre de Laplace once argued that if we knew all the possible antecedent factors of any person's biography, their every act would become predictable (Casti, 1991, pp.53-4). And there is no conclusive argument against this. A person may insist that although there are antecedent factors, their decision (will) is an additional factor. But then we must ask why did they will what they willed when they willed it? 'Whatever may appear to be free within the subjective consciousness of the individual will find its place in the scientific scheme as a link in some chain of causation' (Berger, 1966, pp.142-3).

Determinism is not fatalism. The determinist argues that all events must have causes, and could not be different unless something in the cause or causes was also different. On the face of it, therefore, it looks as though we cannot help what we do. That given all hereditary factors (if indeed they can ever be ascertained), and our present circumstances, and the various external pressures acting upon us, we can be no different from what we are. Detached scientific reasoning endorses the determinist position, yet we obviously act *as though* we are free. So are we merely bio-social automata?

Having scanned the claims of moral relativism, we should look more closely at the now unfashionable idea of those who take a more absolutist stance. It is Kant who laid down the guidelines not only for moral objectivity as a human aspiration, but also for the idea of moral freedom as a human possibility. Kant endeavoured to construct a system of ethics which would permit the kind of moral statement that could be experientially validated, yet was not subordinate to emotions and personal inclination. In other words moral propositions that would command universal respect, and which put duty above desire. He maintained that because humans are subject to irrational emotions and instinctual patterns of behaviour, it was all the more reason why morality should rest on firm foundations and not be subject to facile individual whims. For Kant, nothing was absolutely good except the good will, and he argues that because we all experience conflicts of desire, we should learn to 'universalize our maxims' i.e. do as we would wish others to do.

We are therefore being asked to anchor morality to constraint of an objective kind. And here is the simple but important point: people in different cultures do have different conceptions of right and wrong, but what is most relevant is that they all feel a sense of *ought* about something. It is this universal sense of *constraint* that really matters.

This is the major pointer to the fact of moral freedom. Kant is therefore stressing the existence of an inner, inviolable self which is free regardless of any external circumstances. His argument can thus be seen to have a logical consistency: if we all have this universal sense of ought/ought not which constitutes the essence of moral constraint, then ought *implies can*, the obligation plus the freedom to act, because moral constraint implies moral capacity, and moral capacity implies moral freedom. It can therefore be further argued that *can* implies *must* because moral freedom implies moral responsibility.

In contradistinction to the moral infirmity theme within the classic tradition is that of human (i.e. physiological) inadequacy. In short, the view that humans are somehow: neurologically incapable of being anything 'other than they are. This is how they were born, and this is how they will remain. As long ago as the 19th century, the Italian physician, Cesare Lombroso and his school advanced the notion of biological determinism. On the basis of measurements taken of prison inmates and dead convicts, he came to the conclusion that criminality was due to 'ativism', that is the primitive instincts that characterized humans at a much earlier stage of evolution. This view, which undoubtedly influenced Freud, implies that criminal behaviour especially that of the more extreme kind, was a throwback to the survival instincts of primitive beings which have never been really eradicated.

Such ideas are associated with what has come to be called biological positivism because it relied on what was believed to be the "facts', and therefore not subject to qualifications or interpretation. And although in the eyes of most modern criminologists it is now said to be discredited, it can still be found in the literature – albeit in modified forms, particularly the XYY (i.e. extra chromosome) theory that was popular in the 1960s. (In the past it is known that defence lawyers have tried to get reduced sentences for their clients with the XYY chromosome ploy – though usually without success). It is also represented in the work of neo-Behaviourist psychologist, Hans Eysenck who suggested that criminal behaviour can be positively correlated not only with intelligence, but also with body size.

It is now generally accepted by the experts that biological and environmental causes of crime are closely intertwined; though in what ways they are still not quite sure. It may well be – as some research indicates – that upbringing can leave a physical imprint on the developing brain. Possibly because in some way it affects the limbic system (notably the hypothalamus) in the brain stem which though the most primitive part of the brain is believed to be the human control centre. The front of the hypothalamus is said to 'contain neurons (nerve cells) that promote calmness and tranquility, whereas the back part regulates aggression and rage' although such impulses are restrained by the amygdala (Bylinsky, 1973, p.73). And it is also argued that a malfunctioning amygdala may account for the lack of emotional response to others' (victims'?) feelings on the part of psychopaths who are often immune to any sense of remorse (Carter, 1999). Yet it has to be admitted that the functions of these estimated 10 billion neurons together with their 100,000 or so interconnections which, in turn, receive their 'orders' from the genes is still regarded as so unimaginably complex that even the experts are not able to pronounce with any finality. After all, who has ever located a criminal gene?

Mainly on the basis of experimental work on animals, it has been concluded by some researchers that it is physical anomalies, particularly brain damage that lies at the root of much violent and criminal behaviour. Their argument is that brain abnormalities are to be found in large numbers of the population, and although this does not always lead to violent or criminal acts, it does often account for much delusional behaviour. This is blamed on faulty development in the young (especially up to the age of two during the period of rapid brain growth) which, in turn, is attributed to poor upbringing. Some go further and cite the cause as a lack of affection which they insist is as critical as a lack of nourishment. Researchers have assumed that their work on monkeys reared in isolation shows conclusively that behavioural problems stem not so much from learning difficulties as from 'somatosensory deprivation', in other words, comforting bodily contact. (Note how such ideas have been developed in the Esalen movement, the let's-all-huddle-together therapy which encourages devotees to strip off and jump into the pool together, ostensibly to lose their fears and inhibitions).

Some years ago, again extrapolating from studies of monkeys, psychologist Harry Harlow, at the University of Wisconsin, and neurosurgeon, Dr. Berman of the Mount Sinai Medical School in Brooklyn, concluded that adults with damaged 'pleasure systems' may therefore indulge in violent/criminal acts. Yet at about the same time noted psychologist Albert Bandura at Stanford University came to quite different conclusions. He argued – again on the basis of laboratory research – that criminal and violent behaviour was something that was learned.by example. His work was followed up by that of Robert Liebert at New York State University who came to similar conclusions also based, like Bandura, on research involving small children who were shown to exhibit aggressive tendencies when exposed to films depicting violence. One variant of this was advocated by another University of Wisconsin academic, the eminent psychologist, Leonard Berkowitz, who insisted that mere exposure to offensive weapons such as firearms can trigger aggression in certain kinds of susceptible people. While University of Pennsylvania criminologist, Marvin Wolfgang, veered more towards social conditioning with his theories of criminal subcultures where the young 'inherit' a certain cluster of values, attitudes and life styles – again the notion of criminality by envy and imitation.

Is this all a case of doctors differing or agreeing? Because to some extent all these ideas complement one another, each expert putting the most emphasis where he thinks it is needed. What is particularly interesting, is that few seem to think in exclusively biological determinist terms. Few academics are willing to come down wholeheartedly on either side of the age-old nature or nurture debate. The consensus of opinion is that there may be hereditary traits, proclivities-or whatever (which are virtually impossible to assess), that can be given substance by the appropriate – or in this case, *in*appropriate – environmental conditions.

Yet we still ask questions: what makes people violent? Is there really a criminal mentality? And still there are no very clear answers. So criminologists cling to whatever seems most plausible, and if necessary return to some form of biological reductionism, (note the rather extreme views of William Sheldon in the 1940s in correlating criminality with mesomomorphs i.e. people with a muscular body type). Some years later, Vernon Mark and Frank Ervin maintained that it is no good hoping to rehabilitate violent/criminal individuals through psychotherapy or education, or by sending them to prison, or to improve them by love and understanding, it is a sheer waste of time and will not work.

Such people have some form of biological malfunction, and only when – and if – this is dealt with, is there any chance of changing their behaviour.

Since that time the biological basis for criminality has appeared in various guises (note again Hans Eysenck, 1977 and Mednick and Moffit, 1986). The notion that criminality can be linked with chromosomes (as Cowen, 1979) – really the old XYY thesis all over again which implicates males in particular with aggression – has found new life in more recent years (see Moir & Jessel, 1995) – a text which tries to make clear how biology is a central factor in crime, and how it interacts with socio-economic factors. It also purports to show that over 90 percent of crime is committed by men because the male brain has a lower level of neuro-transmitters responsible for controlling impulsive behaviour. It also puts forward the contentious argument that this aggressive (= criminal?) behaviour can be attributed to higher levels of testosterone. And this, in turn, is linked with the low levels of serotonin found in convicted criminals and which is associated with lack of control of emotional behaviour.

This is really a 'round-up-all-the-usual-suspects' kind of thesis. Not only is a range of chemical substances involved, but they – or the lack of them – are said to be causative factors in a whole melee of criminal types including child abusers, domestic (only?) murderers, psychopaths, rapists and burglars. This sort of thing has to be seriously questioned. It is somewhat like the relative deprivation theory of crime and its attendant weaknesses. We all lack *something*. And it is not that much of a problem to find some sort of deficiency on a post facto examination. It would be interesting to ask how many *unconvicted* people in control groups also fall into the chemical malfunction category, and how many convicted people do not. The truth is that when anyone exhibits strange or uncharacteristic behaviour, it is always possible to discover something either in their personal situation or bio-chemical conditions to which such behaviour can be more-or-less plausibly attributed.

iii) PSYCHOLOGICAL THEORIES AND CRIMINOLOGY

Closely linked with biological theories are complementary ideas which attribute criminality to a minority of people whom nature has apparently endowed with a 'psychopathic personality'. Such ideas are sometimes thought to derive from Freud's teachings, although Freud did not write extensively on crime. What he did do was to stress the power of unconscious drives of which people are not always fully aware, and to insist we are *all* potential deviants, and that it is only the restraints of society that bring us – sometimes reluctantly – into line. Obedience to such restraints both formal (legal) and informal in terms of society's norms is normally learned from parents as part of the socialization process, but – he argued – if this fails or is in some way inadequate, the result may be a withdrawn and amoral individual who refuses to recognise society's rules. In this way – or so it has been argued by many theorists since – society and nature together have produced the deviant which in his/her most dangerous incarnation is the psychopath who is liable to be both conscienceless and violent.

Sociologists (e.g. Giddens, 1991) have pointed out that this entire conception of the criminal has a very limited value. The supporting research has been done mostly on already convicted criminals who inevitably by definition (and 'profession') and nature fall into the deviant category anyway. Furthermore, it can be shown that the character traits most commonly associated with the psychopathic personality can prove to be advantageous in particular situations, as was the case with multiple murderer, Donald Merrett, who also had an exemplary war record in the Royal Navy during the Second World War (Gaute & Odell, 1979).

In trying to discover why people are as they are, psychologists have long recognized that there is a complex relationship between the effects of certain drugs and behaviour. It is known, for instance, that dopamine pathways in the brain can be stimulated chemically by amphetamines. After large doses of the drug, addicts begin to hallucinate in ways some find terrifying. These symptoms – according to some scientists – can be virtually duplicated in forms of psychosis and the not very well understood condition commonly called 'schizophrenia which may also present in types of violent behaviour. An even more common condition – alcoholism – which is also often associated with crime, is likewise not that clearly understood. It too is a complex phenomenon. It may develop initially in response to anxiety and frustration, or possibly conflict and depression, or merely peer pressure – somewhat like smoking which can be immediately addictive. There could even be a genetic predisposition, or some other form of inherited propensity to heavy drinking. Yet when all sorts of rationalizations are taken into consideration, it is also equally obvious that although alcohol is a very potent and health-endangering drug, it is equally obvious that a good many people drink simply because they like it.

Another important ingredient in much crime – especially violent crime – is aggression. But exactly what causes aggression? Again, there may be an ascertainable biological cause as in the case of young Charles Whitman who climbed a tower at the University of Texas and shot everyone within range. Whitman, like so many American children, grew up in a gun-culture (said somewhat unconvincingly to be a legacy of the true American pioneer spirit), but claimed prior to the tragedy that he had 'overwhelming violent impulses'. Yet his aggression could well have been precipitated by a malignant brain tumour which was only discovered at the subsequent autopsy (Davidoff, 1980, p.368).

Psychologists often differentiate between anger-induced aggression and incentive-induced aggression. Anger-induced aggression is an all-too-common phenomenon, and can be generated quite easily over some real or imagined wrong. It may not, of course lead to actual physical violence, but as verbal abuse – as for example, in road rage situations – or merely in the form of menacing attitudes which can be very intimidating. Frustrations, taunts and insults which are themselves the outcome of anger can so easily provoke aggression in the recipient. On the other hand, aggressive actions can result from situations in which there is some conscious incentive. This applies particularly to certain criminal acts, and may well provide the motivation or rationalization for some of the gratuitous atrocities perpetrated in wartime on enemy troops and civilians alike (see Carlton, 1994, and Best, 1998).

Whether aggression is,a natural – possibly survival instinct, or whether it is a response that is learned is still a matter of some debate. It is well known, for instance, that violence and certainly war are virtually unknown in some small-scale societies. But this state of affairs is so rare that it is more in need of explanation that those societies which have recourse to hostilities. What seems to be most likely is that aggression is certainly part of nature, but that conditions of nurture provide the context in which aggression can be expressed. We live in a violent world. When nations are not acting belligerently, the majority of their citizens are getting their fill of television violence. This provides them with the vicarious sensation of violence without the guilt, but doubts persist as to its cathartic value. Why some individuals seem more susceptible than others, and react more peremptorily than others is anybody's guess. The tendency is to relate it to an individual's childhood, but it is really to relate the cause to an unremembered past – a convenient psychoanalytic strategem.

We have seen that some behavioural problems can be attributed to biological factors such as biochemical imbalance or brain impairments of various kinds. These are usually known as organic mental disorders which can include memory loss and general intellectual deterioration which may be caused by injury or disease. Nevertheless, it must always be borne in mind that it is not always possible to relate causally a particular impairment with a particular mode of behaviour. The attempt to do so has often resulted in heated exchanges in the courts where the matter of culpability has to be decided. What the trade terms 'expert witnesses' are not always at one on these matters.

Much more contentious is the question of 'personality disorders'. Indeed, in recent years this has been refined by psychologists, and we are now required to consider certain criminals as sociopaths, i.e. those suffering from an antisocial personality disorder. Such people are said to lack a moral sensitivity, to be manipulative, and to be intent on selfish and momentary gratification. In satisfying their impulses they may not be deterred by the threat of punishment, yet at the same time – so. it is said – they may be cunning, plausible and charming. Unlike those with organic disorders, they may be intelligent and even academically impressive such as the American serial killer,

Ted Bundy, who was resourceful enough to conduct his own defence and escape from custody twice and then elude the police before he was finally caught and convicted in Florida in 1980.

Although the causes of the antisocial personality disorder are said to be unknown, there are believed to be underlying hereditary factors, and it has been noted in some cases that there are certain biological deficiencies. It is reported too that psychopaths (a special category of personality disorder) tend to have weak autonomic responses and be relatively immune to sensory stimulation. Some studies have shown them to be impulsive and excitement-seeking, while others have found them to be suspicious and lacking in empathy. On the face of it, it would seem as though the researchers have got it all ways. They appear to have covered just about every contingency. Their findings taken together could apply to a very large percentage of the population.

So much for the characteristics of those with a personality disorder. But what of the causes? Here again we find that psychologists have made sure that they have covered a range of possibilities, though much depends upon the school of psychological theory involved. Some argue that antisocial individuals may have had too little (or possibly inconsistent) discipline as children. Alternatively, they might be the children of overbearing, highly moralistic parents who just expected too much of their offspring. They can be bright yet cunning children, or they may be (as Lee Robins, 1979) children who have detested school, failed to learn, been obstreperous in class, and been habitual truants.

In summary, we find that the professionals have identified the following traits, tendencies and symptoms in abnormal individuals including those with 'personality disorder':

defective cognitive functioning and self control.

ambiguity of self-image. (It is known for instance, that even those who indulge in petty theft from their firms 'neutralize' such acts psychologically by various exculpatory distancing strategies).

neuroses and possibly psychoses including mood alterations and distortions of reality

anxiety disorders including phobias and panic attacks.

dissociative disorders including amnesia

depressive disorders including possible schizophrenic symptoms (psychopaths exhibit manipulative, self-indulgent behaviour).

On this analysis we all seem to be abnormal in one way or another, and quite a few of us almost certainly share one or two characteristics with the model antisocial individual. How is one to make the necessary distinctions? Must diagnosis always be ex post facto? (it is interesting to note that the barbarous war criminal, Hermann Goering – a psychopath if ever there was one – was also a war hero, and that in his social relationships was found to be genial and good-natured (Overy, 1984).

How valuable, then, are these psychological approaches to the phenomenon of criminology? Either they seem to adopt a 'Molotov Cocktail' approach, giving a whole host of clues and explanations of which one, at least, is sure to hit the mark. Or they insist that one all-embracing explanation can account for everything – the sort of reductionism that one tends to find in psychoanalysis. The implication of all these theories is that the pre-disposing factors are such that the individual is bound to act as he/she does. There is an inner compulsion which cannot be denied – a theory which does have some support in practice. To cite the Bundy case once again: having been convicted of serial murder (he may have killed as many as 40 women) Bundy escaped from prison, but instead of making himself scarce and adopting a new identity, he decided to play a cat-and-mouse game with the police. He seemingly felt compelled. to stay in the area (in Florida, a state which had retained capital punishment) and assault and murder two girls from Florida State University – crimes which finally led to his undoing. Like the 'Yorkshire Ripper', Peter Sutcliffe, he was caught by accident, by a simple police check on his car. He spent nearly ten years on Death Row during which time two journalists, Stephen Michaud and Hugh Aynesworth were able to elicit a somewhat guarded confession from him in which he blamed his crimes on a malignant force which he called the 'entity'. Whether he really believed this, posterity will have to judge, but mysterious evil spirits are by no means unknown as the 'true' culprits in murder cases. (They cropped up, for instance, in the notorious 'Son of Sam' case some years ago in New York, although serial killer, David Berkowitz, had the good sense to disclaim his 'voices' after conviction). Bundy's malevolent spirit did him no favours, and he was executed in 1989.

Although psychologists have generally moved away from deterministic theories of criminal behaviour, the notion of *instinct* still persists in a few shady quarters. It is a relic of Darwinism and had considerable play in Freud's thinking about repressed-sexuality, but except in certain areas of Sociobiology, it is a term that is now rarely used in a technical sense. Although, as we have seen, the notions of 'drive', 'compulsion' and the related – and somewhat more refined – idea of *incentive* are still often used by psychologists in relation to criminal behaviour. However, the idea of instinct is not that far removed from that of anger and aggression. Everyone gets angry, but not everyone becomes aggressive. This is of less interest to psychologists than what they term *predatory aggression* which implies not so much the kind of emotional arousal due to frustration – something of which we are all aware – as the premeditated search for a victim. This is not what specialists refer to as fear-induced aggression or territorial aggression (although these can overlap) but the dispassionate animal-like stalking of a prey is something very much more in line with certain kinds of crime, especially rape and mugging, although these can be opportunistic crimes.

Again we find researchers who are only too willing to attribute aggression to biological factors. In a study of the Qolla tribe of Peru, an American anthropologist found what he, at least, regarded as one of the most aggressive. people known. Brawls were frequent and the incidence of homicide was very high. He discovered that the most aggressive were suffering from low blood glucose (hypoglycaemia), and that this was appreciably lower than other populations that have also been studied. He attributed the Qolla situation to three factors: the effects of living at a high altitude, poor nutrition, and the effects of chewing coca leaves which contain cocaine and tend to deaden hunger pains but has deleterious effects on the body's metabolism (Darley, Glucksberg & Kinchla, 1986). Indirectly, this suggests a theory of behaviour which is induced rather than inherent.

All theories of behaviour, and especially behaviour formation, are inextricably bound up with ideas of how personality is developed. Yet here again, as we have seen, uncertainties abound. Psychologists have not yet arrived at any agreed single representation of personality. True, researchers share certain perspectives, but there is no overall consensus as to how personality is formed. Certainly, the nature-nurture controversy has never been resolved. All are agreed that both are important – it is highly doubtful whether any respected academic comes down fully on one side or another. But no one is sure about the respective contributions of either. There is sound evidence that humans appear either to be born with certain internal representations of the world, or the inherent capacity to form these very quickly. But it is the learning process which undoubtedly gives substance to these inborn capacities, and to make them accessible to conscious analysis.

Having said this, however, it is extremely important – especially as far as criminology is concerned – that psychologists try to develop techniques whereby personality can be assessed. These will not be foolproof, but specialists need rule-of-thumb methods whereby traits, characteristics and proclivities can be identified for practical purposes. Tests have been devised, but as we all know from popularly reported crime cases, in matters of human volition, true – and often tragic – novelties can arise (look how many active and potential paedophiles have found work in children's homes and boarding schools). In theory, tests should possess both reliability, and validity. A *reliable test* is one in which the responses are assessed by comparing equivalent parts or versions of the test. This can be done either by setting alternative forms of the test, or simply by re-testing, and employing more than one assessor. A *valid test* is one where the test actually measures the factors it is intended to measure. Such a test should have a *predictive* capacity (e.g. a person should be hired on his/her capacity to do the work, and not on other extraneous factors – but what if those extraneous factors affect the work in question?) Tests should also have a *construct* validity, that is to say they must provide a system of measures that can be plausibly correlated. (one could imagine a test for anxiety/nervousness in an intending police officer – how would he/she react in a given situation?). The prevailing problem with this type of test is that it has long been well known that people can score well in what they know to be test conditions, but fail miserably in actual situations (see Sorokin, 1954).

With many personality disorders associated with crime, addiction and substance use/abuse come very high on the list. They lead to forms of physical and psychological dependence, and to cravings which can sometimes only be satisfied by recourse to crime. An appreciable proportion of those affected are in low income categories, and find that crime (including prostitution) is often the simplest way of paying for their habit. It hardly needs to be reiterated that for some life becomes a vicious circle of financing and seeking their supplies. The habit can be broken but the pangs of withdrawal are such that some find it virtually impossible. Addiction may be, in John Stuart Mill's words, a 'self-regarding act', but others are necessarily involved, particularly those who cynically profit from the traffic, and who are effectively guilty of manslaughter.

There is no unambiguous profile of the 'dependent personality', but studies suggest that there is a fairly consistent picture of emotional immaturity, (note the case of performer, Janis Joplin), a low tolerance for frustration and tension, and a strong tendency to avoid reality, especially when it is regarded as distasteful. Some addicts almost court disaster by living – either by choice or necessity – in a culture of acceptable abuse (note especially the American jazz scene in the 1950s and 1960s which claimed saxophonists, Charlie Parker, and Tubby Hayes, and overrated artists, Chet Baker and Billie Holliday, besides affecting the careers of numerous others).

Indeed, whether we can say with any confidence that there is such a thing as the 'dependent personality' is very much in doubt. Certainly there are people (personalities) who become dependent/addicted for a whole variety of reasons, not least because ingestion of certain substances in sufficient quantities can create such a dependency. This can clearly be seen in the case of tobacco, a narcotic which some experts maintain is more quickly addictive than heroin. It certainly kills very many more people than the so-called 'hard drugs' (it is estimated that some 300 a day die of tobacco-related disease in the UK alone) and should arguably lose its legal status.

Alcohol too, which, if anything, is more socially acceptable than tobacco can in its own way – be equally dangerous and debilitating, and is much more closely associated with crime. The destructiveness of alcohol can be dramatic and pervasive, in that it can cause serious physical and psychological problems, and in the USA is said to be connected with some 50 percent of murders, 40 percent of assaults and 35 percent of rapes. Again, by no means everyone who drinks becomes an alcoholic (however that is defined). Nevertheless, it is not possible to categorize anyone as an 'alcoholic personality' which implies an inherent – one might almost say, genetic – propensity for alcohol dependency (excepting, of course, babies born of substance-addicted parents who have subsequently to be weaned away from the drug, whatever it happens to be). In general terms, we can safely say that people create their own dependencies – a view that is not always endorsed by some 'progressive' theorists who favour the 'dependency as illness' diagnosis, and would not wish to distinguish between self-induced and other generated conditions.

Another trend closely associated with personality assessment which has enjoyed a limited but intriguing reputation is that of criminal profiling. In the UK, its claims have been modest, but in the USA, some profilers – most notably Robert Ressler – have become well known for their ability to make highly generalized categorizations. Precision is not always forthcoming (the killer will be between 18 and 25 and come from a dysfunctional one-parent family....') and, quite frankly, is hardly to be expected. Ressler is noted not only for his profiling, per se, but also for his interview with serial killers such as John Wayne Gacy (the 'Clown') who is reputed to have murdered at least" 30 young men and Ted Bundy who may well have killed a similar number of women. Ressler admits that Bundy confounded him because he continually re-invented himself and thus presented multiple profiles to the investigating authorities, thus effectively calling into question the entire practice of profiling a particular type of criminal.

After so much work with serial killers – his speciality – Ressler has confessed that in trying to get inside the curious minds of such perverted individuals, and think their thoughts, he feels a real sense of unease. It may be a necessary exercise, but it is also a dark experience which does little for the healthy mental balance of the empathizing investigator.

Empathy is certainly not a characteristic of certain criminals. Prominent researcher, H. Cleckley (1976), suggested that most psychopaths are quite unconcerned for other people's feelings and suffer no remorse or guilt for their actions. They are not indifferent to the prospect of punishment, but are unlikely to change their behaviour in order to avoid it. Indeed, they are quite likely to commit their crimes on impulse, 'because they just felt like it'. But this is not always the case with serial killers, many of whom are plausible and calculating when they target their victims. The particular problem with concocting check-lists of typical behavioural characteristics of the archetypal serial killer (unreliable, untruthful, egocentric, etc.) is that: (a) so many do not fit the prescribed pattern, and (b) some are so aware' of the received wisdom that they can manipulate the situation accordingly. A classic example is that of Kenneth Bianchi and his cousin, Angelo Buono, known as the 'Hillside Stranglers' who tortured, raped and murdered at least five women in Los Angeles between 1977 and 1979. Bianchi, a handsome and charming security officer, had once served as a psychiatric counsellor admittedly on the strength of forged qualifications. But he had done his homework. He went through the normal course of interviews after his arrest, and in addition agreed to be interviewed under hypnosis. In this, he laid the blame for the crimes on an evil alter ego whom he called 'Steve'. Doctors simply could not agree whether he was faking or not. These video taped sessions were shown on TV in 1984, and even experts were not sure whether they were dealing with a psychotic, a multiple personality or what. Eventually they decided not to give him the benefit of the doubt and he pleaded guilty in exchange for a sentence which included the possibility of parole.

We have seen that it is sometimes argued that psychopaths have an unresponsive autonomic nervous system. But if this is true, it is something that is going to be awfully difficult to prove. After all, exactly what is meant by 'unresponsive'? Furthermore, if this is the case, does this imply that their crimes are any less heinous, or that their guilt is somehow mitigated? Similarly, it has been hypothesized that crime – even murder – is their only source of emotional stimulation, but can we therefore say that this in any sense excuses their seeking thrills through criminal acts? No wonder, then, that it is reported that 'typical' psychopaths see little need to change their ways.

It should be pointed out too that various forms of treatment including psychoanalysis, cognitive and behavioural therapy have all had only limited success. Drugs and psychosurgery have also been tried especially with violent offenders, but these too have not been notably effective. Indeed, these have normally only been recommended in the case of those with seemingly uncontrollable outbursts of violence and/or where some form of brain malfunction is clearly evident. Certainly general psychological treatment of whatever variety is sometimes effective with young offenders, but with individuals with long-standing psychopathetic characteristics it remains difficult and uncertain.

Much current thinking favours physiological explanations. Perhaps one day we will even get to the stage recommended by Neuroscientist, Adrian Raine whereby changed behaviour will be effected by treating the dysfunctional elements in the brain (if they can be identified) and removed. The condition is then corrected by inserting the appropriate micro-chips where it matters. Surely the first stage in the creation of the 'bionic-man' – something that will present ethical as well as surgical implications.

iv) THE AMBIGUITIES OF MORAL EVASION

In what circumstances are social norms – particularly the accepted social meanings of deviance – either disregarded, deliberately ignored or conveniently rationalized? In one sense, there is nothing new in this; from time immemorial, societies – and certainly individuals – have contrived good reasons for bad actions. There have always been occasions when traditional norms have been flouted and actions justified. But in modern society an interesting process of value-reversal is taking place: deviance is being redefined as social infirmity or medicalized as some obscure form of human sickness.

Some criminologists, seeking empirical evidence for a possible biological basis for criminality,and unable to detect any identifiable genetic indicators, have turned to the ambiguities of neurology for support. In studies of acute depression and obsessive-compulsive disorder (OCD) researchers have resorted with some success to a technique known as deep-brain stimulation (DBS). This involves invasive electrode therapy to specific areas of the brain which are deemed to be over-active. The entire procedure sounds like a refined form of the much-debated practice of electro-convulsive therapy which is sometimes prescribed for similar conditions. Such techniques are said to yield promising results particularly in cases of 'clinical depression' – an uncertain condition from which two million people are said to suffer in the UK at anyone time (London Times, June 28, 2005).

It is also worth noting that brain scans which appear to depict unusual neuronal activity in patients who have been subjected to various types of visual or auditory stimulation are also interpreted by some researchers as evidence of certain forms of abnormality. But here again it is difficult to know which is the cause and which is the effect. Does the stimulus cause the response, or do the particular nerve centres trigger the behaviour?

When all else fails, and the hypothesized cause of criminal or otherwise bizarre behaviour still proves elusive, it is always possible to redefine the condition. Has the criminal a recognized 'mental illness' -whatever is meant by that term – or, even more nebulously, has he/she a 'personality disorder'? And exactly how are these to be distinguished?

Few cases illustrate the problem better than the Blackwell murders which took place on Merseyside in July 2004. Brian Blackwell, aged only nineteen, was convicted of killing his elderly, prosperous parents after a violent argument over money. He was a cosseted only child who showed exemplary academic promise (four A level A grades) at the expensive (£2,335 a term) Liverpool College, besides demonstrating some athletic ability, especially at tennis. The case almost a carbon copy of another many years before in Somerset both in its motivation, execution and aftermath – began with his unwarranted extravagance over a girlfriend on whom he spent many thousands of pounds which had been set aside for his university fees. The murders had then occurred when the parents had remonstrated with him over plans to take the girl on a holiday to Miami for which he needed their money. Not to be thwarted, he had killed them and stolen their credit cards, and then embarked with his girlfriend on a trip to the USA. It was six weeks before he was finally detained, during which time he had spent £12,500 of his parents' money, and had run up bills of some £30,000.

In murder trials these days it saves both time and money if the defendant is prepared – presumably on the advice of his lawyers – to deny the capital charge, and instead plead guilty to the lesser charge of manslaughter. There was a time when manslaughter charges were normally reserved for those deemed to be guilty of unintentional killings, but it can be invoked for those, like Blackwell, who claim 'diminished responsibility'. But on what grounds? It is here that there is considerable debate. Blackwell – at least at the time of the murder – is said to have been suffering from a 'syndrome' which gave him an inflated sense of self-importance. It was reported that five psychologists (should this have been psychiatrists?) identified this as a 'narcissistic personality disorder', the symptoms of which were a desperate desire for admiration, an undeserved sense of entitlement and a tendency to fly into a rage when frustrated. All of which, to the less technically minded, sounds suspiciously like the tantrums of a thoroughly spoilt child.

So is Blackwell mad or bad? If mad, was it a 'temporary' madness? And what can this possibly mean? Or was it 'cultivated'? There is little doubt that Blackwell was over-indulged by his doting parents. Maybe he was not properly checked and corrected from his early years, or perhaps was and deeply resented it. But it would be a mistake to suggest that the parents conspired in their own deaths. In fact, it is the violent exploitation of their generosity and concern that makes this crime that much more poignant. Their murder was so completely undeserved.

So what really is this syndrome? What are its observed characteristics, and just how are they classified? At the trial it clearly transpired that Blackwell was (is?) a liar and a fantasist. Were even his tears at the trial a matter of shrewd calculation? So to what extent is he culpable? The Diagnostic and Statistical Manual of Mental Disorders recognises certain overlapping personality conditions, including: (i) antisocial personality disorder (ii) narcissistic personality disorder, (iii) borderline personality disorder, and (iv) histrionic personality disorder. All exhibit persistent patterns of what is regarded as abnormal behaviour. In Blackwell's case, the symptoms were identified as exceptional self-regard, an excessive desire for praise and admiration, arrogance and a strong – even violent – reaction to critics, and an unfeeling willingness to exploit the services of others (an 'extreme example' would be the central character of Ira Levin's 'A Kiss before Dying'). Interestingly – and curiously – psychiatrists are still not sure precisely how to treat such conditions.

It sounds as though we are once again in the situation where a description masquerades as an explanation. To name something is not to understand it. These general characteristics can be seen in various forms and to varying degrees in almost anyone. Certainly they are manifested in relevant sets of circumstances. Are we therefore in danger here of medicalising criminal behaviour with spurious scientific labels? It is very tempting to suspect that morality is being supplanted by intellectualized mumbo-jumbo. Psychiatry – and even more its quasi poor relation, counselling – is still very much an uncertain science.

EXCURSUS: ARE THERE 'NATURAL BORN KILLERS'?

In 1994 Oliver Stone's film Natural Born Killers not only raised a storm of protest because of its gratuitous concentration on the grisly minutae of murder, but also because.of its implicit suggestion that some people are born killers. The film opened in the USA in August of that year, and within two months it had been linked with 10 'copycat' deaths including the decapitation of a 13 year old girl by a 14 year old boy who had told his friends that he wanted 'to become famous, like the 'natural born killers'. The film, which came in the wake of Quentin Tarantino's "Reservoir Dogs" and his even more exploitative "Pulp Fiction" (where hit men are seen as the exemplars of 'style'), is believed – despite anti-censorship reservations – to have a malign influence on impressionable psyches.

Predictably, there are those in the academic community who insist that it is impossible to establish any definite causal connection between such portrayals and certain specific events. So was the James Bulger murder inspired by "Child's Play 3", and was the massacre of the people in Hungerford by gun-freak, Michael Ryan, in any way sparked off by Rambo films? Such specific relationships are almost certainly impossible to verify, but there is unquestionably an ethos of easy and acceptable violence in modern society which is certainly not discouraged by such exploitative filmfare.

What, of course, is of complementary concern is the extent to which such media productions have a ready reception among members of the public. Can we easily account for the resonance which violence has with the viewing fraternity? Have we, as a society, become increasingly anaesthetized by the insistent rehearsal of violence – both verbal and physical – in the various media over time? There is little doubt that violence has a ready market, and writers and producers are continually pushing at the boundaries in order to titillate the public palate. Even the dialogue of their offerings with its boorish and offensive language tells it all. (Who ever really thought of hit men as the exemplars of 'style', or 'of obscenity as 'adult' when it is, in fact, infantile and irrational?)

Some will argue that fictional murder by the ubiquitous serial killer is one thing, but actuality is another. But is it? In a North London flat in 2002, Anthony Hardy, who became known as the Camden Ripper, murdered at least three women. Parts of their bodies were found in the flat and in bins nearby.

A recent inquiry has exonerated the North Central London Strategic Health Authority which is responsible for mental health issues from any blame, even though Hardy had a known history of violence. He had been discharged from hospital by a panel of lay managers who had concluded that he was suffering from alcohol addiction and – you may have guessed – a 'personality disorder'.

Belatedly, the chief executive acknowledged that Hardy was 'bad rather than mad', and was not mentally ill in any conventional sense of the term (London Times, September 2, 2005). The powers that be having run out of explanatory alternatives, Hardy was given three life sentences in 2003.

So are there such creatures as 'natural born killers'? Recent research carried out at the University of Southern California seems to indicate that such people do exist. Brain scans were conducted on 41 convicted murderers and compared with those of 41 law-abiding citizens. The tests showed that all the convicts had some damage to those areas of the brain which the researchers claimed were responsible for moderating violent impulses. And it was further hypothesized that this may have been caused by some degree of oxygen deprivation during difficult births. Furthermore, though this could not be known for sure scans are able to quantify the amounts of glucose different parts of the brain convert into energy. The criminals in the tests all exhibited lower than normal amounts, and it was concluded that their brains were therefore not functioning. properly: Research director, Adrian Raine, claimed that individuals with such 'undernourished brains' are less able to cope with violent impulses or to calculate the social implications of their crimes.

The logical – illogical?- extension of this argument, is that it is possible to identity the potential murderer in infancy. If so, it poses an interesting dilemma. What does one do about such children? What precautions could society possibly take in these circumstances? Professor Raine admits that scans cannot tell us everything. There is no absolute certainty that such individuals will turn out to be mass killers. After all, other children have been thus impoverished at birth, and lead reasonably normal lives. Furthermore, one has to take environmental and social conditions into account. Criminality develops because of a complex of factors. Nevertheless, it may be that the malfunctioning brain is one important predisposing factor in the development of violent criminals.

Raine has, unsurprisingly, been criticised by other psychologists who argue that the causes of violent crime are much more complicated than Raine seems to indicate. The motives for murder, for instance, are so varied and exhibit so many nuances that it is just not possible to attribute such crimes solely to brain glucose or oxygen deficiency. Indeed, critics see this as a form of biological reductionism. As we shall see from our studies – most people who commit murder are not violent criminals in the accepted sense of that term. Brain scans in such cases, as some Broadmoor research has shown, do not indicate any significant brain abnormalities.

Raine's work also has some interesting ethical implications. If some sort of screening programme were introduced to identify potential murderers, it could involve a process of 'condemning' certain individuals who had never committed a crime. And this on the dubious, expensively acquired evidence of a brain scan. Few experts doubt that in some – possibly rather rare – instances brain damage of some kind or another is indirectly related to violent criminal behaviour. But most feel that the issue is much more complex than this research appears to indicate.

SOCIOLOGICAL THEORIES AND CRIMINOLOGY

Many sociologists tend to be rather critical of psychological theories of criminality, although the two approaches meet on common ground in the arguably separate discipline (or sub-discipline) of social psychology. And by and large, sociologists are opposed to individualistic and biological accounts of criminal behaviour, and are inclined to favour theories which see social circumstances as the root of the problem.

Historically, sociology has been greatly influenced by the Marxist tradition in which crime is related to the inherent features of oppressive capitalism. It was held – and to some extent is still held – that the effects of poverty and exploitation led to the degradation of the working class and created a 'criminogenic culture'. Later, more sophisticated versions of the same basic theory saw criminality as variously the result of transmitted peer group (sub-cultural) values, and demographic pressure which has resulted in overpopulation which, in turn, has led to crime-conducive living conditions.

This suggests that youths are effectively socialized into delinquency, and where the "gang culture' has developed one can confidently expect crime and criminal attitudes to be perpetuated. Crime becomes a kind of tradition. On this view, criminality is seen as a case of nurture rather than nature although such theories imply that in time the effects of nurture determine the kind of nature. The formative influences of the socialization process therefore become the determinative cause of criminal behaviour.

Closely allied with these ideas is the view that criminal behaviour stems from social dissatisfaction and disillusionment. Such notions were put forward in the early days of sociology by the still respected social theorist, Emile Durkheim who argued that society was characterised by anomie, or normlessness. This is the condition in society in which there is a lack of consensus either about values or goals. The normative structures are lacking, and this has inevitable repercussions at the individual level. Anomie implies that there is a mismatch between the culturally defined goals and the institutionalized (or socially acceptable) means of achieving them. This is well illustrated by the materialist goals prevailing in Thirties' USA and the impossibility that poor Middle West Americans found in the beginning to realise those goals. Thus the rise of the modern bandit in the form of such infamous criminals as Clyde Barrow and Bonnie Parker, John Dillinger, 'Baby Face' Nelson, 'Pretty Boy' Floyd and the Karpis gang whose,bank-robbing escapades were actually applauded by some of the dirt-farming communities who were living from hand-to-mouth. Not that they shared their hastily-won wealth. These were no modern Robin Hoods, but more like counterparts of the old-fashioned Western outlaw in their lethal approach to personal aggrandizement. They created – and for some still retain – a romantic aura which they hardly deserve. But modernity has re-invented them as the archetypal 'primitive rebel' who represents the little man against the otherwise impregnable bastions of capitalism.

The school of sociology known as social interactionism has introduced a theoretical innovation which, quite frankly, is simply a variant of the 'give-a-dog-a-bad-name' approach and is now commonly termed 'labelling theory'. This, as the name suggests, is a theory of attribution. It argues that acts are neither good nor bad in themselves, but – somewhat like the advocates of Emotivism – only possess those qualities which society assigns to them. In other words, normality and deviance are socially defined. It is further maintained, especially by criminologists, that 'negative labels' have inevitable repercussions on the individual's self-identity. Those who are categorized in this way – possibly with good reason – come to see themselves as that which society says they are. So branded, it is implausibly argued, they become the criminals they are seen to be. This is really just another unconvincing form of social determinism. Admittedly it calls into question 'Who labels?' and 'Who gets labelled?' And usually such questions have ideological overtones. But it assumes that individuals are powerless against the forces of the social value system, and further assumes – though this is not often clearly spelled out – that those values are seriously in doubt, anyway. It follows, therefore, according to the social interactionists, that if values are socially constructed, then society has somehow got it wrong. So society itself must be changed and its value system seriously modified – a view that puts the social interactionists to bed with the Marxists. Unsurprisingly, their collaboration in various ways has been quite evident since the 1970s in the form of 'critical criminology'. Radical theorists such as Ian Taylor and Jock Young have been keen to locate the 'real' problems of crime not so much with the individual as with class relations and with the capitalist state. The true villains on this scenario are not the criminals but the criminal justice system and with the courts and policing as a whole.

A common variant is the view that it is not society in general that has got things wrong, but the powerful and the influential (here again we are back with the police and the courts) who impose *their* definitions of crime and morality on others. Crime therefore becomes a function of the power structure of society. The argument goes that most people are happy to go along with these conventions. Sociologist, RobertMerton, long ago wrote of the *conformists* who comprise the majority of the population; the *ritualists* who simply follow the rules as they have always done; the *retreatists* who don't want to know or think about such matters; and the *rebels* who reject such traditional values (See Giddens, 1991, p.128). Impressionistically, one might think that criminals would fall into the last category, but this is not necessarily the case. Many criminals are quite happy to go along with the current value system which is fine for *others*. Indeed, it is the general observation of that system by the great majority that makes criminality possible – *and* lucrative. Without rules there can be no deviance, and therefore nothing that can be defined as crime, in which case criminal behaviour would not exist. But the result would be a general free-for all, except that no society has been known to exist – or, indeed, can exist without rules of some kind or another, something borne out by the uncodified conventions within the most primitive communities.

The whole labelling idea is very little more than a dressed up conspiracy theory. It assumes not only that nothing is intrinsically criminal, but also carries the implication that what is regarded as criminal has been defined as such by the powerful, dominant forces (institutions, authorities, etc.) in society. There is, of course, some truth in this, but it is somewhat less than a half-truth. We all know, for instance, that the law – in certain circumstances – can apply unequally to the privileged and the less than privileged, and that the application of the law can be inconsistent and sometimes bizarre.

One sees this especially in cases of plea bargaining where what is so obviously murder is 're-classified' as manslaughter in order to save the courts time and money. Yet, generally speaking, what the Greeks applauded as 'isonomia' (equality before the law) still applies in modern Western democratic societies.

One of the key problems with sociological interpretations of crime is that criminal behaviour is seen as the – inevitable? – result of determinant antecedent factors rather than something that an individual decides to do. It is seemingly an *inevitable reaction* rather than a deliberate and *calculated action*. But surely those theorists are right who insist that, by and large, crime is a matter of choice. This is the commonsense view. Crime is something in which certain individuals engage because it affords them actual or potential benefits (Cornish & Clark, 1986). We cannot say that most serious crime is not premeditated (the obvious exceptions are certain forms of murder, manslaughter and arguably rape). But whilst acknowledging that some petty crime is opportunist, most serious property crime certainly comes into the premeditated category. But sociologists such as Giddens are surely on unsure ground when they argue that 'the decision to take something from a shop when no one is looking is not so different from deciding to buy a particular product which catches the eye...' (Giddens, 1991, p.132).

Sociological theories are generally useful in that they provide a complementary perspective to psychological theories which stress the importance of personal traits and personality types. They act as a salutary counterweight to those who insist that everything can be explained in terms of individual predispositions. They also emphasise the need to look at the socialization process, and the context in which criminal behaviour develops and flourishes. Such theories are also helpful in the ways in which they categorize types of crime, and in their analysis of systems of law and its application.

But sociology has its ideological agenda. Much modern writing on criminology is concerned not so much with crime as, say, the police would see it, but concentrates on those areas where law enforcement and the criminal justice system are regarded as partial and suspect. Critical criminology takes in issues of race and gender in which discrimination and prejudice, as well as rape and sexual abuse are key issues. Many of these ideas have interiorized the public consciousness and have been manifested in various forms of back-bending political correctness. The murder of Stephen Lawrence and the subsequent litigation following the protests of his parents, illustrates the situation well. The police were unquestionably at fault here and failed both in their investigations and in their inability to bring a successful prosecution. Some colour prejudice on the part of *some* officers may have contributed to the lack of enthusiasm with which the case was pursued – a sin of omission rather than commission. But whether the whole force should be pilloried for what was officially termed lnstitutionalized racism', is very much in doubt. Indeed, on reflection, the idea makes no real sense. And whether the parents should be financially compensated is also a very pertinent question. (How is anyone to be compensated for the loss of a child, except to offset legal expenses? The two are quite incommensurable). And how the boy's father merits an honorary degree for all this, defies commonsense.

Investigation of the social circumstances surrounding crime is particularly pertinent when considering military/political murder, often for reasons of so-called expediency (see Carlton, 1994). This is something we are going to examine in more detail in the next section, but it is worth looking at briefly here in relation to the overall question of sociological analysis. We might think, for instance, about the modes of socialization to be found among 'liberation movements' where children are turned into killers before they are old enough even to appreciate just what the issues are. In Angola, for instance, in 1999, a number of humanitarian aid workers were murdered by Unita rebels for no other good reason than that they represented 'the enemy' – international agencies with a Western bias. Like so many recruits to so-called 'liberation' organizations in various parts of-Africa and other areas of the Third World, the killers are little more than children who feel they are grown-up once they graduate from machetes to possession of an AK47. They are often as ruthless and unfeeling as their older confederates, and think nothing of hacking people to death to save ammunition. The internal politics of some of these countries is such that the consequent disruption and distress is often either unknown or incalculable.

The whole question of conditioning – a subject dear to the hearts of Behaviourist psychologists – is both intriguing and disturbing. For reasons which are not entirely clear, some people are obviously much more susceptible than others. And why some individuals are instinctively drawn to organizations which advocate violence – often in its most extreme forms – and others are not, still defies entirely convincing explanations. In some instances, we know that the motivation is ideological, but this is not always the case as is evidenced by studies of SS prisoners of war (H. Dicks, 1972). Some obviously have what Max Weber termed an 'elective affinity' to certain kinds of movement, cause or programme.

This can be convincingly demonstrated in recruitment to some of America's most militant sub-cultural organizations. Yet even these are dichotomized. There are well established Militia groups intent on thwarting Left-Wing subversion, and who are dedicated to protecting – by force if necessary – what they see as the 'American way of life'. They are stockpiling weapons and supplies in the eventuality that they will have to put their beliefs into practice. Their ranks include a number of ex-service men who advise on weaponry and survival techniques. But to observers they often appear a motley crew, composed as they are of grizzled 'oldies' and naive youngsters all attired in the appropriate fatigues. Traditionally, they have often been at loggerheads with the government, and there have been a number of stand-offs with the authorities in which contestants have been killed. One such was in Idaho in 1992 when a white separatist and anti-federalist, Randy Weaver, engaged in an armed confrontation with FBI agents in which his wife and son were killed.

A more dramatic and widely-reported instance was the destruction of the Branch Davidian sect, a quasi-religious separatist group in Waco, Texas where some 80 members died in the conflagration which followed a government siege. It was perhaps this incident which provoked the horrendous bombing of the government offices in Oklahoma City killing 168 people for which 'patriots' Timothy McVeigh and Terry Nichols were convicted, and caused a dramatic decrease in militia membership. The Branch Davidians and the Oklahoma atrocity constituted a 'revolt' of a different order. They had taken 'patriotism' to new heights of extremism, and had strengthened their resolve with an underpinning of a fervent- if misconstrued – religious ideology. It is just here that it is difficult to draw the line between fairly innocuous Sunday afternoon patriot groups and white supremicist organizations such as the KuKluxKlan, which has spawned virulent neo-Nazi movements such as 'Aryan Nations' which are avowedly anti-semitic and generally racist in orientation. (It was a member of Aryan Nations that recently wounded five people in the Los Angeles Jewish community). However, if we are to keep the record straight – these are equally matched at least in rhetoric – by Black Militant organizations which also adhere to what they believe are clear religious (usually Islamic) principles. It is the more extreme groups of either culture who promote and often practice undisguised violence, even to the point of advocating their own versions of ethnic cleansing.

Militia formations are essentially about power, not so much the power they possess, as the power they wish to retrieve. Theirs is a reaction against what they see as the overarching power of the dominant echelons of society whether they are the organs of government and its agencies, or of monopoly capitalism. Indeed, this whole question of power and how it is exercised is a pervasive theme in the literature of criminology. Authority, in its many forms is suspect, and is therefore subjected to intense critical scrutiny. There is a more than tacit assumption that if we could get behind traditions and divest ourselves of all sorts of ideological baggage we could somehow reform society and retake control of our lives. The basic presuppositions of the critical criminology position is well-summarized by the argument that power 'permeates all formal and official discourses, their language, logic, forms of definition and classification (and) measurement techniques'. And it is exercised through the processes of 'discipline, surveillance, individualization and normalization' (Scraton & Chadwick, 1991, pp.166-185).

It is readily conceded that the dynamics (and 'visibility') of power are not always obvious, and that it is at its intense and its most durable when it is expressed repetitively through regularised and institutionalized routines. But in typical neo-Marxist fashion it is added that these 'are managed through 'official discourses' which derive within the dominant relations of production, reproduction and neo-colonialism. For those – so it is argued – are the determining contexts which reproduce relations of power and knowledge, and it is these relations of domination and exploitation which have been redefined in modern society in such a way that they are seen as justifiable and acceptable in the pursuit of compelling interests.

This kind of class-based analysis is representative of mainstream critical criminology. It is then applied with unequal conviction to criminalization in general, and race and feminism in particular. It is because such groups are seen as socially and economically marginalized that they are therefore said to be prime targets for oppressive treatment by the dominant orders of society. Modern democracies are certainly not all they might be, but are they just a sham? It is surely a gross exaggeration for critical criminologists to insist that while modern democracies maintain the face of consent, 'the tacit understanding is that coercion remains the legitimate and. sole prerogative of the liberal democratic state' (Scraton & Chadwick, op. cit.).

It is worth noting that little is said about criminal and judicial institutions in other unambiguously illiberal societies, especially in the Third World. It is notable that those of the Left are always a little chary about this. Neither is there any plausible suggestion as to what arrangements could be put in place in the liberal democracies (in which theorists are allowed to make their criticisms) which would make for a genuine improvement.

The key word in the critical criminologists' vocabulary is 'negotiation' a much-revered Social Interactionist term. But how is this to work between criminals and police, or within the criminal justice system? There is admittedly inconsistency of sentencing, but is there also too much leniency and too much plea-bargaining, as it is? Or perhaps what they really want is a redefinition as to what constitutes crime. There may still be a little leeway here. But surely not much? (Note the 1990s swing to the Right in American (Republican) politics where George Bush's predilection for signing death warrants for convicted murderers obviously met with the public's approval).

A very similar approach to criminological theories is taken by postmodernists as part of their critique of conventional social values. It should be made clear from the outset that the term postmodernism is something of a misnomer. Its orientations are not even modern inasmuch as they are really a form of old fashioned relativism self-importantly disguised as an avant-garde philosophy. Among its many advocates is the late French academic, Michel Foucault, who in one of his most notable texts (1977) stresses the concepts of 'knowledge' and the given 'order of things' and their influence on the networks of power and governance. These have their own internal logic and contribute as much to oppression as the illiberal intentions of those in authority. His opposition to accepted conventional norms is such that he has been known to say of a multiple murderer that the very barbarity of his crime was an act of resistance against forms of civility. Foucault's emphasis on oppression and regimentation is the keystone of his thinking. For him, the prison was but one 'island' in an archipelago' of disciplinary institutions including schools, hospitals and asylums – not forgetting the workplace and home. Discipline and regimentation are seen as forms of oppression which are justified and policed by a whole cadre of professionals including doctors, psychiatrists *and* criminologists. All are part of the apparatus of social control exercised within the 'punitive city'. To Foucault, a reactionary homosexual who died of AIDS in the 1980s, social control was an obsession. In his own words, 'power is everywhere'. It is probably not too facile to suggest that for him convention and authority militated against his own preferred life-style in 1970s France.

In the argot of the trade, postmodernism has attempted to decentre and deconstruct criminology, as well as much else. It questions the assumptions, rationales, indeed the fundamental paradigms of the discipline. Interestingly, it is those who adopt the radical feminist position who often propose the most extreme re-examination of crime and criminology. Maureen Cain, for example, insists that theorists should go-beyond conventional critical thinking – if that is not a contradiction in terms – and embrace a 'fully post-criminological transgressive perspective.' This neologistic phrasing simply indicates that the writer is anxious that criminologists, especially feminist criminologists, should think more in terms of 'reflexivity, deconstruction and re-construction' (in other words, an open-minded analysis) – her particular concern being the policing of the sexuality of girls and women. For Cain, 'trangressing criminology (sic) is intended to enable women to transgress the binding web of co-man sense'. Whether women – feminist criminologists or otherwise – should insist on defining themselves in relation to men as far as crime and the law are concerned, is a moot point. Rape and sexual assault would seem to constitute special cases, though male to male rape is hardly unknown. Admittedly, most. of those involved in law enforcement and the legal process are men, but it is difficult to think of any crime that is actually peculiar to either sex. So should there even be – indeed, can there be – a separate feminist criminology?

Postmodernists maintain that it is important to repudiate the 'grand narratives' that have previously dominated our thinking. They insist that we must discard the old accepted principles ('referential finalities') which have informed social behaviour in the past whether they concern politics, and, morals or religion. Logic has to be situational logic. Social action must be governed by whatever the situation demands. It must be unfettered by archaic notions of convention or tradition. Everything needs to be re-thought (de-constructed), and the necessary elements re-sorted and re-combined into a coherent whole (re-construction). But could such a deconstructionist discourse have socially devastating effects?

By exactly what criteria is this reconstruction to be determined? What is to be kept in, and what is to be left out? How are we to judge the 'shape' of the new system? Or is there to be no shape – just an ad hoc collocation of liberal ideas to be applied when and how relativistic law-makers think fit?

One of the most difficult tasks facing critical criminologists is how to deal with crimes of state. In what ways can we further refine our ideas of justice (something we will take up in Section 3)? Justice, as a concept, has already passed through the analytical mesh of Sokratic questioning and Roman law, not to mention the agonisings of countless legal pundits since. So how much more is there to do? Or if we take military action as one extension of government policy, can we further refine what is meant by a 'just war'? Can there be 'rules of, war', and in what circumstances can we justify military intervention? And when it comes to what are euphemistically called 'special actions', is it even sensible to ask when an atrocity is not an atrocity? These are very serious issues which should be addressed, even if they are not within the normal compass of criminology as usually envisaged.

EXCURSUS: CRIMINOLGY AND COUNSELLING

Counselling is the new panacea – not exactly a cure-all, but purportedly the next best thing, a console-all form of therapy. Its now difficult to find any kind of disaster, calamity, accident or even a minor unfortunate incident where the victims, survivors, relatives or mere bystanders are not offered counselling. (Its a family joke that I need it every time I have a bath – not one of my favourite pastimes). Needless to say, as a therapy it is now coming to be more extensively used in connection with certain groups of criminals. What was once the almost exclusive preserve of doctors and clergymen has now been taken, over by a whole,array of caring profession diplomates who claim to know how their 'clients' feel, or should feel, in particular sets of circumstances.

Two special target groups among the criminal fraternity are rapists and paedophiles (strictly paidophiles – and not to be confused with pedaphiles lovers of feet, a particularly deviant predilection). These groups consist almost entirely of men, and are usually housed in Vulnerable Prisoner Units (VDU) where they are not at the mercy of other inmates. Many volunteer to take part in Sex Offender Treatment Programmes which are run by a heterogeneous battery of 'facilitators' including prison officers, probation officers, prison chaplains, psychologists and tutors – anyone, in fact, who can confidently claim to act as a counsellor.

Their task is the laudable one of rehabilitation. But does it work? Those who participate are required to make a 'contract' (shades of Behavioural psychology) to the effect that they will maintain certain standards of hygiene, be punctual, complete the necessary 'assignments', and – above all – be cooperative and "honest in their responses. Much of the ritual is performed on a group basis in the highly contentious form of role-play which may be little more than an elaborate game. Imaginary scenarios are one thing – reality is something else. As a form of therapy, or anything else, it is grossly artificial to get offenders to re-enact their crime(s) for the sake of a captive audience. Playing games of 'Old me'/'New Me' in a secluded environment does not exactly inspire confidence in the stated figures for non-recidivism.

One presupposes that most criminals recognize their criminality. Most are unlike the sex offenders whom they tend to despise (hence the reason for sex offenders to be excluded from the regular prison population) insofar as sex offenders often have to be convinced of the gravity of their crimes.

Paedophiles especially tend to regard themselves as abnormally normal i.e. as belonging to an unusual community which is misunderstood by the public at large. What is particularly disturbing, however, is the way in which criminality is often redefined by the more neutral – and therefore less perjorative – term 'deviance'. Some sociologists (and arguably the 'new criminology' is an offshoot of sociology) are prepared to argue that deviance is not to be seen in terms of the quality of the act a person commits but rather as a consequence of other peoples' (i.e. society's) rules and sanctions. Deviance is therefore not simply conduct which requires the attention of those agencies – legal and otherwise – of social control, but merely a label imposed by conforming members of the community. Such ideas, long canvassed by the theorists are increasingly being taken up by the criminal fraternity itself. Criminals are not longer the offenders; they have become the victims of society.

Hence the task of counselling which is intended – albeit in the long term – to make the criminal feel better about himself, to give him a sense of self-worth, and to rehabilitate him for a place in society. He has to be convinced that he no longer needs to feel alienated. What he has done was admittedly- unlawful, but this stemmed from the fact that he was unconsciously rejecting the dominant values of society. This was all the result of some character disorder which the appropriate therapy can hopefully cure. Counselling thus becomes the way forward.

There is a sense in which the pseudo-therapy of counselling is a function of managerialism. Counsellors are 'sent in' by the relevant authorities as and when it is deemed necessary. The cult of managerial ism – promoted principally by that parvenu professional, the management consultant – presupposes that if the organisation is right, everything is right. (How many management consultants, one wonders, have ever been managers?). So the requisite agencies, in our case the prison service and the social services intrude at the appropriate level.

It used to be said that 'the customer (client) is always right'. This is no longer the case. Now it is a matter of the professional – the patron – who knows best. So they 'send in the clowns'. *They* know how *we* feel. Bereavement Counsellors – who may never- have been bereaved themselves – know what the bereaved are experiencing.

Medical Counsellors who have never had cancer, know just how to console the person who has just been given the fateful diagnosis.... and so it goes on. Except for any practical advice about facilities, etc., anything they say is usually superfluous. (Even support groups such as, say, Victim Support, have a limited usefulness insofar as there is a tendency towards a system of multiple monologues instead of dialogue).

What is even more worrying is that anyone can try it – and many do. A short course (or possibly no course at all) will suffice to equip the would-be counsellor for the work. What are mainly required are 'listening skills' and the ability to reflect back the responses in such a way that the clients effectively answer their own questions. How helpful can such techniques be in dealing with criminals who have no gnawing sense of remorse? Indeed, can a sense of remorse be generated? For those who are genuinely repentant, the prospect of rehabilitation is already reasonably certain.

What are the basic presuppositions of much counselling therapy? The range is. enormous and can apply as much to criminals as to such way-out organizations as the Re-evaluation Sisters (motto: 'Its great to be female') a movement for the liberation for oppressed fat lesbian women?

i) everyone is born with unrealised intellectual and moral potential.

Furthermore, everyone has a capacity for 'lovingness' and zest for life, but these qualities have become 'blocked' in adults as the result of accumulated 'distress experiences' involving fear, anger, loss, pain, embarrassment, etc.

ii) possibly this has been exacerbated by a social ideology (perhaps endorsed by parents or peers) which discourages showing one's feelings or any indication of wimpishness.

iii) recovery may be possible by a process of confiding to one's counsellors, or in extreme cases by some form of 'emotional discharge' (crying, trembling, rage, laughter etc.). This may free individuals from rigid patterns of behaviour, and help them to realise their 'basic cooperative, loving and intelligent nature'.

This entire farrago of quasi-humanistic rhapsodizing is not really supported by the evidence. Experience cannot substantiate the optimistic view that high intelligence, lovingness and so forth can be said to be the 'real nature' of men and women. Nor can it be established – regardless of certain forms of neo-Freudian theory – that virtually all our problems stem from the half-remembered traumas of youth. Furthermore, it can be cogently argued that so-called distress experiences may be a source of self-realization and self-determination. So is the universal value of fortitude and resilience to be discouraged? 'Emotional discharge' can be rather like the impermissible temper tantrum of the child which makes them more objectionable. And confiding may become little more than the maudlin recital of personal thoughts/grievances which only serve as one more source of boredom for others in the group therapy class. Or it may give occasional titillation to the counsellor who might actually be slightly contemptuous of clients who are seemingly incapable of resolving problems for themselves.

The 'Its good to talk' injunction, so beloved of telecommunications companies, may have a limited usefulness as an aid to moral regeneration. Certainly the role of the professional counsellor is in doubt except as a possible source of practical. information. How much is counselling likely to influence inveterate criminals let alone ruthless killers? And how much can it really console the victims of their crimes, especially the bereaved? And where counsellors assume any other functions (perhaps by usurping those of the clergy whose advice should, at least, have a spiritual dimension) it is an act of presumption. Counsellors purport to be intent on 'empowerment', but, in fact, divest individuals of the capacity to sort out their own lives.

SECTION 2

A typology of murder

(including case studies)

INTRODUCTION TO A TYPOLOGY OF MURDER

It is extremely unusual for social scientists (including criminologists) to admit to the reality of evil. As we have seen social science writers tend to 'explain' evil in terms of psychopathology and sociopathology and no doubt they would refer unsympathetic enquirers to theological texts if they insisted on viewing crime in such unscientific terms. Critics would argue that evil and good are human constructs and therefore exist only because society has said they exist, and that in fact conceptions of good and evil are culturally relative. Even in our own society they can be seen to have changed over time.

Yet, having said this, there are some values which seem, as near as possible, to be universal: honesty, truthtelling, justice, loyalty, etc. Similarly, there seem to be crimes which are generally regarded as so heinous that they have incurred near-universal disapprobation. Murder, in its various forms, is probably the most common of those crimes.

It is important, however to distinguish between murder and killing which is usually associated with warfare where, in theory at least, killing is politically justified – something we will need to examine. The distinction may seem casuistic but it is a necessary one. This can be seen from the controversy surrounding the 'Bloody Sunday' incident in Northern Ireland in 1969. The case has undergone successive examinations and re-examinations. Catholic agitators were certainly killed by members of the Parachute Regiment who claimed that they were under serious attack. It is still not clear just how serious that attack was, and whether the soldiers were in any real danger. To date, the bias of evidence has indicated that the Paras over-reacted, but in the circumstances it is still arguable that this was a case of killing rather than murder.

It has to be admitted, however, that there are occasions such as in the case of atrocities where one shades into the other. And when it comes to wholesale, mechanized murder such as the Holocaust, few people would disagree that here we are in the presence of evil – however this is to be defined (Sereny: 1991). It has, of course, been argued by revisionists that the industrialized massacre of the Jews and others was no worse than the destruction of Dresden, Hiroshima and Nagasaki by the Allies, but at least this was, done *as part of the war*. Terrible as they were they contributed to final victory, this cannot be said of the Holocaust programme or of the systematic ill-treatment of prisoners of war by the Japanese.

In this section, therefore, we are going to look at murder and its many often confused – motives. Case studies will be used, though not in the same way as in Tennyson Jesse's early but still classic text, Murder and its Motives. In these it is hoped to demonstrate the adequacy or otherwise of some of the theories we have been considering in Section 1. Some of these studies will already be known, although a number will be relatively unfamiliar. In particular, they will show that the murderer is no one kind of a person. It is highly disputable that murderers are born as unusual persons with defective genes. They may not even be confined as a class to those people who happen to be characterised by the established cluster of psychopathic traits such as narcissism, deficient emotional responses and so forth. Indeed it is the contention of this text that we all share these characteristics to a greater or lesser degree. Undoubtedly, there are truly exceptional individuals who are, as Jeffrey Dahmer's father said of his son 'both sick and evil'. But most murderers are very ordinary people caught up in extraordinary situations in which they choose an amoral alternative which they may then seek to justify. Nowhere is this better illustrated than in the history of persecution and atrocity. Wasn't it Lieutenant Calley (whose group of well brought up Americans committed the dreadful massacre at Mailai in Vietnam) who said nonchalantly afterwards that 'it was no big deal'.

i) MURDER FOR REVENGE

It cannot be overstated that many murders and near murders (as in our main case study here) have been motivated by the desire to inflict maximum injury on a person or persons because of some known or assumed harm done to the perpetrator.

A somewhat atypical case in which revenge was the attributed motive was that of William McDonald, a British ex-serviceman, who committed four murders in Australia between 1961 and 1962. The victims were all male vagrants in the Sydney area, and all suffered multiple stab wounds and mutilation of the genitals. The police quite naturally – and correctly as it turned out – suspected an anti-homosexual motive. The killer who was dubbed the 'Sydney Mutilator' was caught quite by chance. He was a postal worker, an immigrant, who claimed that he had been the victim of a homosexual attack while serving in the British Army in 1944. This, he claimed, had been such a traumatic experience that he had been subsequently diagnosed as a schizophrenic and discharged from the Army, after which he had spent periods in various mental institutions. After emigration to Australia his mental condition continued to deteriorate – though why this was not detected by the immigration authorities earlier no one seems to know. When he was questioned, McDonald said that he heard voices that inspired him to murder and mutilate – a claim (or ploy) that has been made by many others accused of multiple murder. His plea of insanity was accepted in mitigation by the court, and although sentenced to life imprisonment, he was in due course committed to a centre for the insane.

The crux of McDonald's case was the claim that the homosexual assault many years before had been so traumatic that it had changed his personality; A very similar case has been made for T.E. Lawrence (of Arabia fame) by some of his many biographers. In this instance, it was a homosexual rape by Turkish guards while in prison during the First World War. Again there has been the suggestion that this was so dramatic that Lawrence never recovered from the experience. Indeed, it has even been announced that – like the transforming bite of the vampire – it either turned him into a homosexual or confirmed his own latent homosexuality. In the McDonald case, we are asked to believe that the result was just the opposite, he felt compelled to take revenge on those he regarded as sexual perverts. Though one is forced to ask why it took so long to take effect. Whatever, he obviously had the sympathy of some of the jury in what was a typical case of attribution. Horrendous as his crimes were, some people could imagine that they had a certain kind of distorted rationality. And he probably fared a great deal better than a comparable heterosexual murderer whom, we may suppose, had been seduced by some women while still a teenager and had then victimized other women.

Disturbed marital relations can often generate such hatred between estranged couples that violence leads to murder. It is often said that love and hate are different sides of the same coin – an adage that is well exemplified in the Jo Ann Wilson case in 1983. Forty-three year old Ms. Wilson was shot dead in her garage in Regina, Canada by a man who was seen fleeing from the scene. A credit card receipt which it was assumed had fallen from the man's pocket was found lying in the snow. The signature was that of the murdered woman's former husband, Colin Thatcher, a very wealthy Canadian businessman from whom she had had an extremely acrimonious divorce. There had also been bitter arguments particularly over the custody of their three children which further exacerbated the situation.

A previous attempt had been made on Jo Wilson's life in 1981 when an unknown assailant had fired at her through the window of her house. And it became known that Thatcher, who was a highly respected minister in local government.in Saskatchewan, had spoken to his current American girlfriend about the possibility of hiring a contract killer to do away with his former wife. And when he did locate a potential assassin, a police surveillance team monitored the proceedings, but obviously did not intervene in time to save her. Thatcher was arrested and put on trial in October 1984, with his erstwhile girlfriend acting as a prosecution witness. He was belligerant in court, claiming that the whole thing was a frame-up. His bad impression on the jury, and what proved to be damning circumstantial evidence resulted in a verdict of first degree murder for which Thatcher was given a life sentence. He had obviously been brooding obsessively for some time about the injustice of the divorce, and eventually out of sheer hatred he had arranged for his ex-wife's death, and in doing so had sacrificed wealth and a particularly successful career.

In the Thatcher case there was no question of attribution – the motive was clear. Likewise in the main case study here, where the motive was spelled out in correspondence by the perpetrator whom it took many years to identify.

Threats against commercial and industrial organizations for the purpose of extortion are well known, but rather less well known are campaigns of intimidation for the purpose of revenge. One such case which did not actually result in murder, but which might well have done so was that which involved a series of bombings at the Consolidated Edison Company building in New York. The first bomb was found in a tool-box on a window sill of the building on November 16 1940 with a note which said simply: "Con Edison crooks, this is for you". Given that such a note was wrapped around the bomb – a fairly crude affair – it was assumed that it was intended that the bomb should be found before it exploded. The bomb was small, and the incident did not generate much public attention. But this was to change as the bombs – some 30 in all grew bigger, and the campaign of the man dubbed the 'Mad Bomber' continued for another sixteen years.

The police really had nothing to go on. The notes – of which there were many – had no fingerprints and the bombers 'signature', the technique used in the bombs' construction, could not be matched with that of any other known bomber. The Consolidated Edison Company supplied much of New York's electricity, and it was obviously assumed that the criminal was an ex-employee who had some kind of a grudge against the company, The second bomb was discovered a year later lying in the street stuffed in a sock. The alarm-clock mechanism was, not wound, and the police guessed that the bomber had been on his way to the Consolidated Edison's headquarters in another district of New York when he had been interrupted or scared off for some reason.

Within three months, the USA was at war, and a note was received at police HQ which informed them that the bomber was not going to continue his campaign for the duration of the war because of his 'patriotic feelings', but that later he would 'bring the Con Edison to justice.... for their dastardly deeds'.

The letter was signed F.P., and from 1941 to 1946 at least sixteen other letters were received by Con. Edison, The New York Times, various theatres, department stores and hotels containing the same signature. Needless to say, the vast majority of those concerned instantly dismissed the letters as the work of a disenchanted crank. And for the next four years nothing more was heard from F.P.

In March 1950, however, a third unexploded bomb was found at New York's Grand Central Station. It was put together in a more sophisticated manner than the previous two, yet the police recognized that it was still the work of the same person. But the fourth bomb the very next month did explode, as did the fifth a few months later, but fortunately no one was hurt in either explosion. The sixth and seventh bombs, both at the Con. Edison building, did not go off. More ominously, the eighth which also did not explode, was found tucked into the seat of a cinema where the upholstery had been cut for the purpose. It is anybody's guess what would have happened had it worked.

By this time, the police may have entertained some doubts as to whether they were really dealing with the same person, then just before the New Year (1951), the New York Herald Tribune received a letter which again cited Con. Edison, and suggested that the company was responsible for the bombers continuing ill-health. Again, it threatened cinemas, and as usual it was signed F.P. Soon afterwards the office of the Journal-American received an angry phone-call from a man identifying himself as F.P. He accused the press of largely ignoring him, and threatened that they would regret it. He was determined that the justice of his 'cause' should be recognized.

Of the bomber's first eight 'units' (as he called them) only two had worked, but the next four more expertly-made bombs all worked. They exploded in the period 1951-52, and were larger and thus much more dangerous than his earlier efforts. In this phase, there were injuries, and the media at last realized that these were not isolated incidents. There was a 'Mad Bomber' at large. In 1953 there were four more bombs, all larger than before. More people were hurt, and its a wonder no one was killed as one explosion sent shrapnel flying through the famous Radio City Music Hall. This must have given the bomber some satisfaction. He had now found his own peculiar kind of fame, and he should know – he was there at the time.

In 1955, the pace accelerated. In a period of approximately twelve months there were six bombs, two of which did not explode, although one in Grand Central Station nearly killed a military policeman. By

1956, the police were still baffled. The Consolidated Edison Company were still looking at their old files in the possibility of turning up some clues as to which disgruntled ex-employee might be taking revenge in this rather bizarre manner, but without success. Even the public by this time had detected that there was obviously some connection between the company and this prolonged series of outrages.

During 1956 more bombs were set. One in the famous Macy's Department store injured several people. And another – a variant of the usual pipe bomb design was found in a telephone booth in the RCA Building by a guard who, in ignorance, took it home where it blew up his kitchen at two o'clock in the morning. Letters still deluged the press. The bomber was becoming increasingly frustrated with his own lack of notoriety, he railed against being called a psychopath and threatened more bombings if Consolidated Edison was not 'brought to justice'.

The largest bomb yet was left in a cinema in December, and when it exploded it injured six people, three of them seriously.

It was at this point, after several people had already been maimed and the bomber – according to his subsequent confession – had set 54 devices, that the police decided to step up their investigations and called in the services of Dr. James Brussel, a psychiatrist, who was also Assistant Commissioner of the New York State Department of Mental Hygiene. He was a noted specialist who had also served with the US military.

Dr. Brussel (from whose records much of this material is derived) unsurprisingly, diagnosed that the bomber – whoever he was, was suffering from paranoia. Brussel defined paranoia as a chronic disorder of insidious development characterized by persistent, systematized and therefore logically constructed delusions. The assumption is that once the central premise of the paranoid person is accepted everything else falls into place. It constitutes a logically consistent system. By believing that other forces are ranged against him, the paranoiac becomes increasingly introverted, self-centred and defensive. This, in turn, may seek compensation in a delusionary sense of self-importance and superiority.

Next, Brussel – venturing into the uncertain realms of criminal profiling – suggested that the bomber was middle-aged, and that according to earlier studies the chances were that he would be of 'symmetrical' (well-proportioned) build. It followed too from the neatly printed letters and the meticulous preparation of the bombs that he was an orderly and fastidious man. He was probably too a person who otherwise deplored what he saw as bad behaviour, and may never have been in trouble with the law. Moreover, when in work he had almost certainly been an exemplary and conscientious employee. Brussel also surmised – rightly as it turned out – that the phraseology of the letters suggested that the man was probably of foreign extraction and possibly largely self-educated. But was this simply adventitious ?

This all seemed reasonably persuasive – even to the police. But it was then that Brussel began to betray certain Freudian influences. He had noted that all the bomber's capital letters were perfectly formed, except one – W. Instead of forming it as a double V, it was written as a double U. Um, thought the psychiatrist, this looks suspiciously like a scrotum or possibly a pair of breasts; perhaps we have here a man with (unacknowledged ?) sexual problems. His prognosis then became even more bizarre. Why did this meticulous man slash cinema seats to plant some of his devices? Could this indicate rape and penetration or even castration? Brussel came increasingly to see sex, frustrated or otherwise, as the key to the problem.

It would seem that for psychiatrists nothing can be as it seems. The obvious is suspect – after all, that would make life too easy. There has to be some hidden motivation. So this man couldn't just slash seats in order to hide a bomb. One must seek out the 'hidden logic' behind the action. So Brussel began to toy with the quite unverifiable notion of the Oedipus complex. The bomber's hypothesized love for his mother must have prevented him from maturing sexually. The seat slashing must -either symbolically represent the penetration of the mother or "the castration of the father – or both.

At this point, Brussel's imagination began to run riot. Perhaps the bomber was unmarried – maybe even a virgin – because his mother was the only person he had really loved. He probably lived alone, communicating with very few people, and solitarily brooding on his grievances. Quite possibly he was a Slav – after all, Slavs in recent history, at least, have been associated with some bomb outrages. And if he was a Slav he might also be a Roman Catholic who maintained his mental equilibrium and his lack of a sense of guilt by regular Confession. Maybe too he was a sick man, perhaps suffering from some chronic illness believed to have been brought about by the stresses of work. A man hungry for attention who might be sub-consciously longing to be caught – perhaps in order to air his grievances more publicly, and to let those who saw him only as a lonely little man know who he really was.

The police took the risk of publishing a summary of Brussel's analysis in the hope that it would provoke some reaction. There were the predictable hoaxes: cranks and weirdos, and those who were intent on leading the police on a fruitless merry-go-round. Consequently the police were engaged in one wild goose chase after another. Meanwhile, the search at Consolidated Edison went on in the hope of locating one of their possible 'victims', but their efforts were complicated by the fact that the company had been involved in several mergers since its establishment in the 1930s.

As if to throw down the gauntlet to the police, the bomber placed two more devices in public places, a library and a cinema, both of which did not explode – indeed, perhaps were not intended to. These were followed up by a threatening phone call to Brussel himself – perhaps the psychiatrist's profile was not that far wide of the mark, after all. In a parallel development the Journal-American challenged the bomber to give himself up, but this resulted in a contemptuous reply. This was followed by a further letter in which the bomber again complained of years of injustice which he felt entitled to avenge.

The Consolidated Edison Company were still ploughing laboriously through their earliest files, especially those concerned with injury compensation, when one of their employees came up with the name, George Metesky and the expression "dastardly deeds". His was not a specially noteworthy case. The file contained letters which indicated a not unusual argument between an obviously disgruntled Metesky and the Company over the amount of compensation he had been awarded, but the case had been finally settled without obvious recriminations as long ago as 1937. Apparently Metesky had been employed by a Consolidated Edison subsidiary from 1929 to 1931, and had been hit by a backdraught of gases from a boiler which he claimed had given him headaches. He spent some time at home still on the payroll, and later his employment was terminated. It was not until 1934 that he filed a claim for permanent disability on the grounds that the accident had left him with tuberculosis. The claim was unverifiable, and anyhow was filed too long after the accident. There was copious correspondence over the next three years, and after apparently accepting the company's decision, nothing more was heard of Metesky.

The file looked so promising that the police Bomb Investigation Unit decided to follow it up. Metesky's work record indicated that he had been an exemplary employee, never insubordinate and always trustworthy. Nevertheless, a discreet enquiry was made in the rather run-down district where George Metesky (originally George Milauskas) lived. It turned out that, as per the profile, he was middle-aged and unmarried, and he lived with his two older sisters. He was unemployed because of chronic illness, and so far he had no police record. It transpired that although the family appeared to live blameless lives, neighbours regarded them as strange and unfriendly. When questioned, Metesky gave the impression of being polite and cooperative – but he admitted nothing. But then made the self-confident mistake of writing again to the press and citing the critical date of September 5 1931, the day of his accident, thinking – so he later admitted – that it was so long ago that the police would not be able to make anything of it.

When he was finally arrested, Metesky was courtesy itself. He showed the police his workshop (even to the point of showing them the parts for his next bomb) and enlightened them as to the initials F P which he said simply stood for Fair Play. When the press were informed, the whole thing naturally became front-page news, and Metesky positively revelled in his newly-won notoriety.

Metesky had- actually been born in the USA in 1903. He had joined the Marines a little after the First World War and had been trained as an electrician. The only work he had done since his accident had been a stint at a tool factory during the Second World War. Although assured by doctors that he had not got TB, and that such an accident could not cause tuberculous, Metesky insisted that he knew better – and eventually it transpired that he was right. When tackled about the bombs, Metesky was adamant that he had not intended to kill anyone. He protested that his bombs were much too carefully made: Eventually, he was committed to a hospital for mentally ill criminals. He was a model patient, and spent his remaining years trying to secure his release by legal means, because – true to type – he believed he should never have been there in the first place.

ii) INTENDED MASS MURDER FOR PROFIT

On Wednesday September 24 1952, an explosion occurred on a Douglas DC3 aircraft flying between Mexico City and Oaxaca. It transpired that a bomb had been placed in the forward baggage compartment with the general intention of killing everyone on board, though with the *specific* intention of killing certain people only. The' fact that specific deaths would necessarily entail the deaths of many others was merely incidental. Very fortunately the plan didn't succeed. The aircraft landed safely, and although several people were hurt in the explosion, no one was killed. A very thorough investigation was carried out, and the police uncovered a mass of evidence which implicated two men, Emilo Arellano and Paco Sierra. The prosecution was able to trace the purchases of the bomb's components and the tools used in its manufacture. They established that although Arellano had actually made the device (he protested that all he had constructed was a 'box' not knowing what it was for), it was Sierra who had initiated the deadly scheme. In court, each man tried to blame the other, but only succeeded in incriminating themselves still further.

The case was a very protracted affair; the record itself ran to seven volumes. It was 53 days after the questioning of the witnesses that the prosecution delivered its summation, and another 53 days before the defence lawyers did likewise. Such was the procedure under Mexican law at the time. Both men were found guilty of attempted murder and insurance fraud although there was a considerable disparity in the sentencing. Sierra received eight -years from one judge and thirty years from another, while Arellano received the maximum sentence of thirty years.

Arellano was a trained engineer who had also studied chemistry and who had already taken out two modest – if ambitious – patents. He was one of a large family, and in interview stressed that he had been brought up to observe 'high moral values'. He was separated from his wife, and they had reared two children, a daughter and a son who had since died. When questioned he claimed falsely to be a 'graduate engineer' and protested that as an 'expert' any bomb he had made would have done what it was intended to do – the implication being that the DC3 device was the work of an inefficient amateur. 'If I had wanted to kill twenty people, I can tell you that there would not have been a single splinter left of that air plane, (Larkin: 1959, p.103). He disclaimed any knowledge of any 'beneficiaries' who were named on the incriminating insurance policies.

Interestingly, the interviewer, a journalist, hazarded the opinion that if Arellano was guilty as charged, he 'must have been cold and blind to the sufferings of 'others from his earliest years' (op. cit. p.98). Of course, such hypothesized deformities of character are rarely detectable at an early age. Yet it is an assumption that some like to make because it tends indirectly to separate murderers from 'normal' people as though all murderers are a breed apart. There are truly exceptional cases where psychopathic tendencies can be identified in childhood, but – by and large – murderers are ordinary people in whom the potential has become actual.

Paco Sierra, the co-defendant, was a very different proposition. He was a polished, fastidious man who came from a relatively prosperous family from which one day he hoped to receive an inheritance. Although he had worked in the accountancy department of his father's firm, he had also had some musical training and made his debut as a singer when he was in his early twenties. His studies were furthered by his concert tour partner whom he subsequently married. Later he graduated to opera and to radio, achievements of which he was justly proud and – some might think – inordinately vain. For the last ten years, however, he said he had concentrated on his wife's career, and insisted that he had enhanced the business interests which had been initiated by her second husband many years before.

But this was not the whole story. Their entertainment business had apparently not been doing too well for some time. There was a large outstanding mortgage on the theatre which Sierra had actually planned to increase even at an interest rate of twelve percent – hardly a sign of financial health. He also insisted that his business acumen had been such that he was able to 'save' his wife's jewels which he claimed were heirlooms that were worth a fortune.

This was all grist for the defence case in that it supported Sierra's claim that he had not – and didn't need to – participate in any fraudulent enterprise. As he put it, in interview, 'I have no need of a fantastic plot to kill people in order to make a living. I was in the midst of large negotiations when I was interrupted by this miserable affair. I was forming a company of Mexican talent to take to Cuba. I am still young, I still have my voice, I have my position as a leading impressario...' (op. cit. p.123). Furthermore, he said he had ambitious plans for a funeral scheme (a high priority for devout Catholics) which would benefit ordinary workers who would pay this insurance by small additional contributions to their Unions. This money-making scheme had been concocted with Arellano who, said Sierra wishing to distance himself from his fellow-accused – was not really his 'friend'. According to Sierra, this grandiose idea never successfully materialized because of Arellano's mismanagement.

To complicate Sierra's case, there was some evidence that he had fathered the child of a young woman who once in court would neither admit nor deny her involvement with the would-be entrepreneur. Could this be the reason that he urgently needed money? Sierra also would neither confirm nor deny the affair, he magnanimously insisted that he would die rather than 'reveal the name of a woman who had given me her body in love' (op. cit. p.127).

Sierra protested his innocence, arguing that his apparent guilt turned on a series of odd coincidences. He argued that Arellano had sought to involve him in the crime to divert attention from himself. But Sierra still couldn't adequately explain the insurance policies in his possession. Details told against him. He was not as prosperous as he had claimed, and there persisted a deep suspicion that even his marriage to an older woman had been contracted mainly to get his hands on his wife's money and property. And once convicted he shrewdly suggested to Arellano that if he would absolve him of the crime, he would do his very best to get Arellano's case reviewed and his sentence shortened. It was an obvious ploy. There was absolutely no guarantee that once released Sierra would do anything of the kind.

Once in prison, Sierra, who, as a celebrity, was treated extremely well, suddenly went on the rampage, possibly (so it was thought) in a fruitless attempt to feign insanity. By simulating madness he may have been hoping to be transferred to a private institution. But as time went by it became apparent that something was really wrong, and that he was suffering from mental delusions.

In June 1956, the Supreme Court met to re-consider the cases of both Sierra and Arellano. There was much dispute' in Sierra's case, but no doubt about Arellano whose thirty year sentence was confirmed. As far as Sierra was concerned, much was made of his previously unblemished record and his one-time fame as a singer. The outcome, however, was unsatisfactory. There was to be a compromise, he would serve somewhere between eight and thirty years. After all, both had tried to kill twenty people.

One tries to understand just what brings individuals to the point where they are prepared to carry out such an atrocity as this. It might be said in Arellano's favour that as a boy his family had been uprooted by the Mexican revolution, and they had been forced to move to El Paso which was noted for its anti-Mexican sentiments. He had obviously dreamed of one day striking it rich by one of his 'inventions', but nothing had succeeded, and it may well be that he bore a grudge against those who failed to recognize his 'genius'. As for Sierra, he had received modest but flattering applause for his musical gifts, but in the long term his abilities had not brought him the fame and riches he craved. He had married a woman getting on for twice his age – again, possibly out of acquisitiveness. It was an arrangement which ultimately proved unsatisfactory, hence his liaison with an untutored servant girl.

Both men were greedy, but hardly the 'undeveloped human beings' as seen by their interviewer. They were characterized by a certain naivete, and a false sense of their own ingenuity which was probably their eventual undoing. But nothing in their biographical profiles can possibly excuse the outrage that they very nearly carried out.

There have been a number of other cases like this one, some of which have been successful – if that is the appropriate term – and some not. In April 1950, for example, there was an explosion on a British European Airways Viking aircraft en route from London to Paris. It tore ragged holes in both sides of the fuselage and destroyed the amenity departments besides damaging the rudder and elevator cables. None of the passengers was hurt, but a stewardess was quite seriously injured. The incident was thoroughly investigated by New Scotland Yard, and it was concluded that the explosion had almost certainly been caused by a bomb, although no tell-tale fragments were found. There were no arrests, but one is left wondering who were the intended victims.

In the same month in Los Angeles, an aircraft technician tried to plant a suitcase containing a petrol bomb into a plane bound for San Diego. But a baggage-handler dropped the case which promptly – and prematurely – caught fire. It turned out that the technician, John

Henry Grant, had insured the lives of his wife and two children for $25,000. His motive was both money and the desire to marry another woman, a fatal combination which netted him a 20 year sentence for attempted murder.

In May 1953, there was a second Mexican incident. It happened at the village of Mazatlan when the luggage of an aircraft on the La Paz flight was being taken to the main building. Two of the baggage handlers and the airport manager were killed, and fourteen other people were injured. Investigators found fragments of a clock – the timing device – and evidence of dynamite in the remains of a package which had been sent from the town of Culiacan. The sender had almost certainly intended the package which weighed 77 pounds to go by the shorter route across the Gulf of California, in which case the remnants of the plane would have disappeared in the sea. As it was it had been dispatched on the aircraft taking the longer route via Mazatlan.

The investigators found themselves enmeshed in a situation which could have come straight out of a crime novel. Who were the intended victims? All the passengers on the direct flight were questioned, and eventually a man was detained whose appearance corresponded with that of the description of the person who had sent the package. Suspicions were confirmed by the fact that the same man had tried to hang himself in a public park before being apprehended. Jose Alfredo del Valle confessed that with the aid of an accomplice he had tried to simulate his own death so that his widow could collect the insurance. He further admitted that he had got the idea from the Arellano-Sierra affair, and had practised making bombs for nine months having secured the equipment from some unwitting military friends. He was convicted of murder and sentenced to serve thirty years in prison, but being apparently wracked with guilt, he successfully committed suicide on the third attempt by taking a huge overdose of sleeping tablets in October 1956.

The first recorded case of sabotage of an aircraft by means of a time bomb occurred in May 1949 when a converted Army C47 owned by Philippine Air Lines en route to Manila from Daet exploded and plunged into the sea less than a half hour after take-off. The crash was witnessed by a fisherman off the coast of Luzon, and he testified that the tailplane had sheared off, but that the main fuselage was not on fire. The plane, which carried four crew and nine passengers, sank to the seabed, although one or two fragments floated to the surface. On the basis of their investigations, experts concluded that this was no ordinary aircraft failure; the evidence pointed to a bomb in the luggage compartment.

Three men were charged with sabotage and murder. The main culprit was Crispin Verzo, a maintenance man at a local cinema, who was said to be enamoured of his boss's wife – significantly his boss was one of the victims. Verzo's accomplices were small-time criminals who were prepared to help for a modest remuneration; whether they had been taken into Verzo's confidence at every stage of the plot is not really known. This was reflected in the sentencing. All three men were sentenced to death, but after an interminable five years, the Supreme Court confirmed the death penalty for Verzo, but commuted that of the conspirators to seventeen years four months. There was considerable support for Verzo among his fellow workers, and before the final date set for his execution, April 5 1958, he had already received eleven reprieves. On that very morning, the President commuted the sentence to life imprisonment.

Was there some lingering doubt that he had been shielding someone else'?

Two classic cases in which the murderers were intent on destroying a plane in order to kill specific people regardless of all the other passengers were those of J. Albert Guay in Canada and John Gilbert Graham in Colorado. Both men were intent to kill those individuals to whom they were related; the fact that very many other people were to die was of little consequence to them – their deaths too were merely incidental.

Albert Guay wanted to marry someone else. So why not divorce? Well, he also needed money, so why not make a vice of necessity? He had toyed with the idea of killing his wife for some time. He had already considered – and rejected – several methods including poison and blowing her up in a taxi cab (for which he had tried to enlist the help of a friend). But after reading the account of the Philippine disaster, he finally decided it was to be a bomb on a plane. He even took his girl friend on a flight, stopwatch in hand, in order to study the terrain where the 'accident' might be staged. He was naturally anxious that it should occur over water where the remains of the plane would presumably be lost.

Guay was a jewellery salesman, and he was able to enlist the help of a watchmaker friend to construct the bomb, and to get the watchmaker's sister to purchase the necessary components. They made several tests, then once the date was fixed, Guay took his wife on a 'consolatory' week's holiday. And on the very day that he took out the $10,000 insurance policy, he treated her to a trip to the theatre.

The bomb was put aboard a Canadian Pacific Airlines DC3, in September 1949 and twenty minutes after it took off from Quebec, it exploded killing 23 people including three children. But Guay had got his timing wrong. The aircraft crashed over land, and the tell-tale bits of.the bomb were recovered.

Guay and his accomplices were soon arrested and questioned separately (as part of the interrogation he was taken to the scene of the crash and apparently wept hysterically). All were found guilty; Guay made a full confession and he was executed in January 1951, and his co-conspirators in 1952 and 1953.

In November 1955, a United Airlines Mainliner with 44 persons on board exploded just eleven minutes after leaving Denver, Colorado. Investigators from the Civil Aeronautics Board were soon at work, and they discovered that the explosion had been caused by a bomb placed in the rear cargo area. The case was turned over to the FBI, and a fortnight later they arrested John Gilbert Graham the twenty-three year old son of Daisy Graham, one of the passengers on the ill-fated aircraft.

Graham made a complete confession to the police, and told how he had made the bomb which he had placed in his mother's suitcase, using some or all of the twenty-five sticks of dynamite which he had recently purchased with the sabotage plan in mind. He had taken out an insurance policy on his mother's life – a policy which was actually worthless because his mother had failed to sign it. But he had also persuaded her to make a will leaving him her drive-in restaurant should anything untoward happen to her.

At his trial which lasted three weeks, he refused to take the stand and testify on his own behalf. Similarly, he would not allow his young wife to testify, nor would he entertain his court-appointed attorney's plan to enlist the services of a psychiatrist who would presumably have made some reference to his 'emotional sickness'. Certainly, the story of his background suggests that the young man was unhinged in some way or another. Even when he was sentenced to die in the gas chamber, he waived his right of appeal and asked that 'the verdict be carried out with all convenient speed'.

Perhaps the whole story will never be known, but there were enough clues to indicate that for whatever reason he had an inordinate hatred for his mother, although it is said that he was her favourite child. As a youth he had forged cheques in her name to the tune of $4,000. For this he was convicted but was paroled from a five-year prison term. In fact, his mother was still in the process of paying this money back at the time of her death. He had even abandoned a truck belonging to his mother in the path of an oncoming train, and had arranged a gas explosion at the drive-in restaurant for which the insurance was collected.

Graham apparently showed no remorse for his horrific crime, but he was concerned that people should know about his disadvantaged childhood, and how he had been temporarily placed in an orphanage by his mother after she had been widowed. Although he had returned home when she had remarried, it seems to have been an experience which caused lasting resentment. Could this really be said to constitute 'emotional damage'? And is such damage irreparable and therefore exculpatory? Indeed, before going to the gas chamber in January 1957, he is said to have rejoiced at his mother's death.

As a footnote, it is worth remarking that the Federal Government decided that because certain states have abandoned the death penalty, this kind of crime which often involves a crossing of state borders, should be classified as a federal offence. Given the enormity of such crimes, they might well be therefore considered as capital offences.

iii) MURDER FOR GAIN

A whole gamut of crimes patently come under this heading. It is – and possibly always has been – one of the commonist motives for murder, remembering of course that there are different kinds of gain. And murder for gain can take place in all kinds of different circumstances from, say, the slow poisoning of a relative to secure an inheritance to the impulsive shooting of a shopkeeper in pursuit of a robbery. The former, a calculated act, once almost always merited the death penalty as in the case of Daisy de Melker, a nurse who poisoned two of her husbands for the insurance, and her son who was becoming a dangerous nuisance. She never made a confession, but was hanged in 1932. On the other hand, what was almost certainly an unintended murder in the course of a trifling theft resulted in the execution of the perpetrator, eighteen-year old Francis Forsyth, who had kicked his victim in the head. This also involved the execution of an accomplice, Norman Harris, who although guilty of assault had not delivered the fatal blows, and raised again the old problem of 'equal responsibility' before the law.

Here we are going to look at several cases, some of which are not that well known, and others which pose interesting questions about the application of the law.

A favourite and deadly terrorist contraption is the pipe bomb which can be easily and cheaply made, yet they are often very effective. In the history of crime, however, they have certainly not just been the special weapon of terrorists. In 1985 in Naples, Florida, the pipe bomb was the chosen device of one man who was intent on maintaining a luxurious life-style. Steven Benson constructed two quite sophisticated bombs which were detonated remotely, killing his mother and her grandson in her Chevrolet car. Her married daughter who was standing nearby was also seriously injured.

Margaret Benson had inherited a great deal of money from her husband who had made a fortune in Canada in the tobacco business. They had owned a number of properties in the D.S.A. and Canada as well as several cars – in short, they had all the trappings of affluence. After her husband's death, it was clear that her son expected a generous share in the inherited wealth. He engaged in a number of business ventures which failed, and at first his indulgent mother was prepared to make good his losses. But when it became obvious that he had misused a loan which his mother had made for him to start his own electronics firm, she made it clear that nothing more would be forthcoming. She had no intention of supporting him any longer, and actually demanded the repayment of the loan and even indicated that he might be excluded from her will.

Steven Benson may have been something of a waster, and obviously had no head for business, but he enjoyed his luxuries, and showed considerable, ruthless ingenuity in trying to ensure that he was going to continue to live in the manner to which he had grown accustomed. But he wasn't quite ingenious enough. He left fingerprints on one of the bomb casings which he assumed would be totally destroyed. He was soon arrested, tried and sentenced to fifty years' imprisonment. The final irony was that under Florida law he forfeited his eligibility to inherit his mother's remaining wealth.

The unpremeditated murder is well illustrated by the D'Antiquis case in April 1947. Three masked men attempted a robbery in daylight at a jewellers in London's West End. All three were armed, and one actually attacked the shop's manager. But things didn't go according to plan, and the gang were forced to make a quick getaway. As they rushed out of the shop they were seen by Alec D'Antiquis, and as he drove his motorbike into their path, one of them shot him in the head at point blank range. In a panic, they left him dying in the street while they disappeared into the traffic. Among the many eyewitnesses to their escape was a taxi driver who saw two of them run into a building in the Tottenham Court Road. The police carried out a search of the building and found a discarded raincoat and a scarf which had been folded to make a mask. The revolver was also discovered later on the foreshore of the Thames, and ballistics proved that it was the weapon that had killed D'Antiquis. But it was the raincoat that was the clinching factor. It was eventually found to belong to twenty-three year old Charles Jenkins who already had a criminal record. The two accomplices, Geraghty and Rolt, were soon arrested and both confessed, implicating Jenkins whom witnesses had failed to identify.

All three were convicted. Terence Rolt, still only seventeen was 'detained at his Majesty's pleasure', but Jenkins and twenty-one year old Geraghty were duly hanged in September 1947. This case highlighted yet again the debate about the death penalty, partly – in this case – because the criminals were so young, and partly because it was seen as a wildly impulsive act of desperate men. Yet it could also be argued that D'Antiquis had also been bravely impulsive in trying to foil their escape, and had been brutally slain for his trouble. Britain had just emerged.from a war in which many very young men had been killed; most of the public were not going to lose too much sleep over the execution of young thugs who had needlessly slaughtered a courageous citizen.

However, this and many similar crimes beg questions about those who can kill without blinking, as it were, especially when the killers are young and often ill-educated. Such crimes are not infrequently committed without any compelling motive, and are senseless in that they are perpetrated for trivial reasons – if, indeed, there is any reason at all. Fairly typical would be one of the many – almost incidental – murders committed in New York in any one year. A body was found in the roadway at Central Park West at 3.0 a.m. on one very cold morning. The body was blocking traffic, and even at that early hour, small groups of curious onlookers were gathering, as they so often do at a crime scene. The body was identified as that of Herbert Holtz, a man in his thirties, who although shot twice in the back appeared not to have been robbed. It had first been spotted by a Naval officer and his girl friend who had heard the shots and had seen a man running out of the park. The police contacted the dead man's twin brother, Leon Holtz, who said that Herbert was a quiet man with, no criminal associations, and added that he worked for Metro-Goldwyn Mayer, and could only surmise that his brother had been shot 'by accident'.

There were no other witnesses and no obvious clues; all detectives could do was to work through the dead man's address book in the hope that it would give them a lead. This was a laborious business, and entailed questioning dozens of people, many of whom were said, euphemistically, to be of the Bohemian-chichi variety. Forensics established that the gun used was an Army issue.45, but enquiries at government arsenals produced nothing. In short, after several days the investigation had all but petered out, though it was still technically on file.

Three months later, the investigating team got their first real lead. They had a call from officers at Staten Island who said that they had a prisoner who claimed to know something about the Central Park murder. The inoffensive looking young man was Robert Hoag, arrested as a member of a gang of hold-up specialists, who was obviously intent on buying favours from the police. He was prepared to talk about the murder providing his girl friend was in no way implicated. The police made no promises but were prepared to listen (he explained that the girl-friend was married to someone in the Army – 'you know how it is'). Hoag told the detectives that another member of the gang, John Scheer, had taken the automatic which others used on various heists, to 'get some dough'. When he had returned in the early hours of the morning he was in an agitated state and said that he had 'killed a guy'. It transpired that Scheer had already been apprehended in Brooklyn on other charges, and after initial denials, finally admitted the killing. The motive, he said, was simple, the man (Holtz) was a homosexual and had made improper advances and he had shot him 'to get rid of him'.

Had any man really wanted to solicit this seventeen year-old with 'lank blond hair, a wispy fuzz on his drawn cheeks and numerous pimples'? The officer in charge of the case – admittedly a not unbiased source – actually referred to his 'ill-arranged body' as something not quite real (Keating & Carter, 1956, p.49). After further coaxing, Scheer confessed that he had primed the automatic and gone out with the intention of robbing someone. It was *he* that had approached Holtz with a view to divesting him of his money, but the man had shouted and started to run away, hence the quite unnecessary shooting. This was corroborated by friends of Scheer who knew about the killing and who readily conceded that Scheer had an 'itchy finger' as far as guns were concerned.

Scheer was indicted on a charge of first degree murder, and predictably an array of probation officers was in court to testify to the youth's early difficulties. His mother had died when he was an infant, and he had been brought up by his father and grandfather both of whom were classified as 'stern disciplinarians' (the suggestion here, of course, is that the boy lacked the ameliorating love of an understanding mother). But from early years he had displayed pathological tendencies, torturing animals – cutting off cats' tails being his speciality. He was expelled from school twice for truancy and was arrested when he was fifteen for stealing a car. Since that time his father had reported him to the police for being completely incorrigible. Other charges had followed, and from then onwards it had been a downward spiral into petty crime.

Scheer had no money for lawyers, so those appointed by the court tried to get the charge reduced from Murder One to Murder Two, but the prosecutors wouldn't wear it. As one of them said, 'What are we – a social welfare agency?' In their estimation, Scheer was a loser, a waste of social space, and they regarded it as something of a defeat when he was finally given a life sentence and not the electric chair. The District Attorney's Office had its batting average to maintain.

Several years later there was, if anything, an even more senseless killing in New York during a hold-up, this time at the Hotel Greystone. According to witnesses, a young man had tried to hold up the hotel, and had met no resistance either from the night manager or the employees. The takings were meagre. He was given some cash from a drawer, and the employees were required to empty their pockets and hand over what little they had. Then the youth noticed a filing cabinet, and demanded the key. When the night manager, Harold Morris, quite truthfully said that he didn't have the key, the young man in his frustration simply shot him and walked out.

The following afternoon, the police received an anonymous call telling them that the assailant was one, Robert Kelly, and that he lived in a furnished apartment on the West Side of the city. When the police arrived there, the young man said that his real name was Robert Brown, and made no attempt to deny the charges. Like Scheer, he was a sickly – almost wasted -looking youth who was also a night-time habitué of Times Square. Though unlike Scheer, he was not awkward or belligerent, even though he'd had an equally chequered boyhood. He didn't know who his parents were, and had been brought up in a series of institutions and foster homes. From early years he had been in trouble of one kind or another, and had in fact been paroled from a Reformatory (where he had served two years of a one to ten years sentence for armed robbery) only six weeks before the Greystone affair. Before the Reformatory episode be had actually joined the US Marines, a notoriously tough and unforgiving outfit, from which he had unsurprisingly deserted.

The charge against him was much the same as Scheer, but the outcome was likely to be more serious because he was older (he was twenty), and there were eyewitnesses to the shooting who would confirm his guilt. He had also been found with watches stolen from the hotel's employees. So it was an open and shut case. Even the probation report did him no favours. While making some allowances for his unfortunate childhood, it made clear that he was rebellious and aggressive, cynical and lacking any kind of social or ethical values. However, a writer from the New Yorker unexpectedly took an interest in the case. He delved into Brown's background and found what he believed to be one or two mitigating factors, for example, that he had spent much of his life looking for his mother, and trying to locate any relatives he might have.

But how convincing is it to be told by one psychiatrist that the young man's emotional yearning for his mother could 'explain' his senseless criminality?

The possibility of reducing the charge was hardly felt to be one that the public would accept. The night manager had also been young, was a war veteran, and had left a pregnant widow. Yet the prosecutor still had to take the psychiatrist's report into consideration. This had strong Freudian overtones in its emphasis on Brown's powerful mother-fixation. But exactly how can one plausibly argue for a causal connection – even a strong correlation – between Brown's pathological criminality and paranoid delusions stemming from an overwhelming mother-fixation? Some will still find this baffling. Needless to say, it was another case of when doctors differ. A different psychiatrist refuted the defence doctor's thesis, and pronounced Brown legally sane. Nevertheless, yet another death was seen as indefensible. Brown was saved from the death sentence.

Just how much early experiences can in any sense justify subsequent criminal behaviour is still a matter of some debate. Closely related to this issue is that of the brutalizing effects of early custodial sentences. For example John Dillinger was given a ten-year sentence for an unsuccessful unarmed robbery in 1922 (of which he served nine years). He was just twenty-one at the time of this his first offence. Within a year of his release in 1933 he was branded by the FBI as Public Enemy No. 1. By this time he had made two daring escapes from prison; his gang (of which two were later electrocuted) had netted some $300,000 from bank robberies and had killed eight men including some police officers. Dillinger himself was shot to death in a 'G-Man' (government man) operation after being betrayed by a brothel madam.

The question is: what would have happened had the young Dillinger been treated more leniently in the first place? He obviously learned the rudiments of his trade in prison where he also recruited the principal members of his gang. Like so many other criminals, he was no ignorant thug; he was both intelligent and – according to contemporary reports – quite personable. We can, of course, never know what might have happened if his energies could have been directed into more constructive channels. Given the old adage that it takes one to know one', he might have made a good government agent himself.

But what of a different kind of murder-for-gain; that of the methodical and calculating poisoner? In some ways, the poisoner is the most complex and intriguing of murderers. In contrast to crimes of momentary passion and violence, the murder by poisoning suggests studied premeditation extending in some cases over weeks and even months. The cases we are going to consider are not particularly famous, they are not quite in the Herbert Armstrong (executed 1942) or Frederick Seddon (executed 1912) category, but they are instructive nevertheless. Two things are worth noting briefly about poisoning cases. First, that their hey-day was in the 19th and early 20th centuries, perhaps because in those days the possibility of detection was less likely, especially where obscure poisons such as aconitine (as in the Dr. George Lamson case in 1882) and antimony (as in the Dr. Edward Pritchard case in 1865) were used. Second, poison as a weapon has traditionally – though not entirely justifiably been associated with women (as in the Louisa Merrifield case in 1953). Understandably poisoning has suited some women (note the Dorothea Waddingham case in 1936) because it requires no physical strength, only nerve – or in some cases, a certain degree of ignorance as in the Charlotte Bryant case also in 1936. Perhaps one further point should be made about the choice of poisons. Generally speaking, a poisoner sticks to the substance he/she finds most effective. But there have been exceptions. The infamous Dr. William Palmer (executed in 1856), another in the community of medical murderers, liked variety and was prepared to use strychnine, opium, etc., whatever came to hand as long as it would kill.

To keep the balance right we will take four cases from each of the key centuries, two involving a woman, and two involving men. In 1882, Louisa Taylor was thirty-six. She had just become the widow of a pensioner who, by definition, was a good deal older than herself. She then lost no time in looking up two elderly friends of her late husband, Mr. and Mrs. Tregillis, and soon became their lodger. Both the Tregillis', despite their age, seem to have been in reasonably good health, but very soon Mrs. Tregillis became so ill that a doctor had to be called. The patient had a certain blackening of the teeth itself an unusual and somewhat suspect symptom – and was said to be suffering some degree of dementia (then categorized as 'senility'). However, it was felt that the elderly lady could be left in the capable hands of the younger woman.

Mrs. Tregillis' health fluctuated over the next few weeks. At times she seemed to rally, only to sink back into a state of complete exhaustion. Her husband was completely puzzled. But it was known that he had spent some time in what was then termed a mental institution, so no one took that much notice of his growing suspicions about Mrs. Taylor. Not even when he saw Mrs. Taylor wearing his sick wife's clothes, or when she suggested that they might go away together, regardless of the fact that his wife lay seriously ill. Failing this, Mrs. Taylor, managed to persuade him to hand over his meagre pension.

This was all too much for Mrs. Ellis, the landlady, who was party to much that was going on, and she called the police and invoked the services of the doctor once again. Mrs. Taylor was charged with theft, and shortly afterwards with causing the death of Mrs. Tregillis by lead poisoning. The medical evidence was conclusive. Louisa Taylor was found guilty of murder and hanged early in January 1883. Her motive was certainly not a consuming passion for the feeble and confused Mr. Tregillis, but for his pathetic nineteen shillings a week pension. A similar motive may lie behind the death of Louisa Taylor's late husband, but his body was never exhumed in order to confirm this.

Several poisoners of yesteryear have dispatched their victims with strychnine, a substance with particularly horrible effects. It was used, for instance, by the notorious Dr. Neill Cream, who killed several prostitutes in 1892. Unlike some poisons such as morphine (the favourite weapon of multimurderer Dr. Harold Shipman) the victims of strychnine poisoning suffer excruciating pain and very agonising deaths. The case in question is little known now, but caused something of a stir in the aftermath of the First World War.

Ethel Brown was the only daughter of a Lincolnshire gamekeeper. As a young woman in the early years of the last century, she became pregnant – not an easy matter to face at that time – and never revealed the name of the father. The child, a daughter, was brought up by her parents and passed off as her sister not that unusual in the circumstances. (It is probably only an incidental fact, but of the eight women hanged for murder in Britain between 1923 and 1955, five of them had what were then termed illegitimate children. This is a somewhat higher figure than the law of averages would suggest, and may indicate certain class factors).

Arthur Major had known Ethel Brown as a schoolgirl, but in 1907 had later moved away to Manchester. In 1918, they met again, and after several meetings they were married shortly before the end of the war. It was perhaps an extremis exercise for both of them. She was twenty-eight with an illegitimate daughter a fact she didn't disclose. Moreover, given the high casualty rate in the war, she was fortunate at her age to find a husband. He, on the other hand; was a veteran who had been very seriously wounded (he still had over twenty scraps of shrapnel in his body), and he had also been gassed. In this poor physical condition he was discharged from the Army in 1919 with less than enviable prospects. However, he managed at first to get work as a gardener, and despite his infirmities was able to father a son in whom he appears to have taken little interest.

Life was difficult for 'many in the early postwar years. The Majors moved about, living in labourer's cottages depending on where Arthur Major could find work. Fortunately, they were able to rent a small bungalow at Kirkby-on-Bain, and it was here that someone told Arthur Major about his wife's 'immoral conduct' and about the 'sister' whose true status had never been revealed. This understandably – was the first in a sequence of incidents that finally led to murder.

There was now an atmosphere of resentment and anger. Ethel Major still refused to say with whom she had previously been intimate, but then it probably would have made little difference if she had. Her husband constantly accused her of being immoral and deceitful, yet he in turn – possibly as a form of retaliation – began seeing another woman. He also resorted to alcohol, which besides being no solution at all, was an indulgence he could ill afford. Nevertheless, the precarious relationship continued in a state of slow deterioration until May 1934. It was then that Arthur Major first showed signs of being seriously ill. It began with a severe headache; then came the trembling, the foaming at the mouth, speechlessness, and then the tell-tale indications of strychnine poisoning, uncontrollable convulsions of the body. His son was duly alarmed at this 'mysterious illness', and a doctor was called who initially thought it might be epilepsy. But his wife dismissed matters by telling the doctor that her husband had fits from time to time, though no one else seemed to know anything about it. He then appeared to recover a little, but within twenty-four hours the convulsions had started again. He was just able to drink a little water which his wife brought him, but exhausted by the pain he lapsed into unconsciousness and died. His wife did not contact the doctor, as might have been expected, but instead quickly called in an undertaker. Subsequent opinion had it that she wanted her husband interred as soon as possible.

A death certficate was duly issued; it appeared that no one at this stage had any suspicions that the death was anything but heart failure brought on by acute epilepsy. But someone did have doubts because the coroner received an anonymous letter to the effect that a neighbour's dog who had been seen eating scraps put out by Mrs. Major, had also been found dead. The coroner passed the letter to the police who ordered an examination of the dead dog, and also arranged for Mr. Major's burial to be postponed. In July, Mrs. Major was arrested and charged with the murder of her husband, but it was not until October that her trial was held at Lincoln Assizes. The jury heard a great deal about the friction in the Major household, and about Arthur Major's heavy drinking. But they obviously felt that the most incriminating facts spoke for themselves. They were out for just one hour, and found Mrs. Major guilty, although they added a strong recommendation for mercy. The plea was ignored by the Lord Chief Justice at the Court of Appeal, and Ethel Major was hanged on December 19, 1934. The irony is that whatever her motives she murdered someone who trusted her; apparently her husband's last words to her, reported by her son, were, 'Don't leave me – you have been good to me'. How good he never even guessed.

In our next case, the motive was quite unambiguous – it was one of barely concealed greed. Forty year-old Frederick Seddon had a 'responsible position'. He was a district superintendent with the London and Manchester Industrial Assurance Company. He lived in Islington with his wife and five children plus an aged father, but as if this was not enough to contend with, in 1910 he decided to take in a lodger. Eliza Barrow, by all accounts, was not the easiest person to get along with, neither was she particularly astute. But she had money, and Seddon made sure that she should be relieved of all her financial worries by gradually acquiring her assets which were exchanged for an annuity. This gave her a weekly income of £3 a week, which at that time was certainly more than the average wage.

Before long, Miss Barrow became ill. A doctor was called when the symptoms became very acute, but it was all too late and within two weeks she had died. Seddon arranged for the funeral, and made sure that it was as inexpensive as possible, and even managed to get a small commission from the undertaker for giving him the work.

None of Etiza Barrow's relatives were at the funeral simply because Seddon had thought it prudent not to inform them. Her cousin only learned about her death when, on the off-chance, he had visited the Seddons. When questions were asked about the dead woman's property, there were only evasive answers. The only clear statement the cousin received was that Eliza Barrow had made everything over to Frederick Seddon.

The whole affair looked very suspicious. The cousin, Frank Vonderahe, went to the police, and an exhumation was ordered. The forensic results were undeniable – the woman had died of arsenic poisoning. All this took time. But three months after the onset of Miss Barrow's illness, Frederick Sed don was arrested, and his wife several weeks later. They were tried at the Old Bailey in 1912, and Seddon was found guilty but his wife was acquitted. Seddon had hoped to influence the judge by giving him an esoteric Masonic sign, but His Honour, though a member of the brotherhood, was not impressed. Seddon was hanged on April 18, 1912, having vehemently protested his innocence.

The Barlow case in 1957 is interesting more because of the method than the motive. On the night of May 3 in Bradford, Elizabeth Barlow was found dead in her bath. Her husband, Kenneth Barlow, a male nurse, told the doctor – and later the police – that he had been dozing in a chair and waiting for his wife to come out of the bathroom. On awaking he decided to investigate, and found his wife unconscious lying under the surface of the water. He said that he emptied the bath, and tried to revive his wife by using artificial respiration. Having no success, he ran to his neighbour and asked them to call a doctor, then returned to the house to continue his attempts at resuscitation, but it was too late, his wife was dead.

At first, the doctor was puzzled. It did not look like a case of 'normal' drowning. Why hadn't the victim tried to haul herself out of the bath? The body showed no signs of violence, although the doctor did notice that the pupils of the eyes were widely dilated. But on closer examination, he detected, small puncture marks in the buttocks. Later, the police did find a number of hypodermic syringes and needles in the house, though this did not strike them at the time as being especially unusual in the home of a nurse. Nevertheless there was enough prima facie evidence to arrest Kenneth Barlow on a charge of murder.

Although Mrs. Barlow had died in May, the trial did not begin in Leeds until December. It was a complex case, and a great deal of preparation work had to be done before the Crown could proceed. Not least of the prosecution's problems was the question of motive. No one could fathom why Kenneth Barlow should kill his wife who was pregnant at the time. Elizabeth Barlow was his second wife, and they had been married for less than a year at the time of her death. And then there was the matter of method. It was the Crown's view that he had murdered his wife by an injection of insulin. But there seemed to be no firm medical evidence to support this, although certain positive tests had been carried out on mice which seemed to indicate insulin as the particular agent. In court, Barlow admitted that he had given his wife several injections of ergometrine in an effort to procure an abortion. This, he insisted, was not his wish but had been done at his wife's request. He denied that he had ever given her insulin, the symptoms of which would be quite different from those of ergometrine.

Witness evidence at the trial pointed in both directions A neighbour testified that the Barlows seemed to be a happy couple and that Kenneth Barlow gave every impression of being a devoted husband. But two people who knew him professionally recalled conversations in which he had mentioned that one could commit the perfect murder with insulin because it was so difficult to trace. Further medical evidence brought by expert witnesses of the prosecution supported the view that although the cause of death was drowning, the coma had been brought on by an overdose of insulin. Yet as a counterweight, the defence's expert witness insisted that an increase in insulin may have occured naturally as a result of a rush of adrenalin brought about by the sudden fear of drowning. The respective experts became locked in a technical debate which was never quite resolved. It was the first case in Britain in which a murder was said to have been committed by the use of insulin.

The judge ruled that everything turned on the medical evidence. It was either a case of murder or nothing. The jury took only an hour and a half to decide that it was murder, and Kenneth Barlow was sentenced to life imprisonment, although he steadfastly maintained his innocence. The question of motive was never resolved, but there were murmurings about the inquest on his thirty-three year old first-wife who was said to have died of undetermined 'natural causes'. Presumably Kenneth Barlow had *something* to gain, but only he knew what it was.

EXCURSUS: MURDER, SHAME AND REMORSE

The discussion here is not so much about murder as self-murder. It follows the view of those who argue that there can be no greater evidence of real remorse for the crime of murder than for the murderer to be so grief-stricken that he/she commits suicide. It hardly needs to be stressed that many criminals feign remorse or simulate repentance if in some way it can be to their advantage, such as a lighter sentence or special consideration for parole. Of course, suicide may follow murder simply because the offender cannot face the prospect of endless years incarcerated in prison, but, as far as one can make out, this is not usually the case.

It can be argued that cultural differences can determine the ways in which murderers legitimize their crimes – something which the acute observer has noted has not been helped by 'enthusiastic jailhouse biopsychiatrists' (Leyton, p.216:1997). But, by and large, shame and remorse tend to be related to early internalized value systems, and – as we shall see – often result in an inability to function after the crime However, it is important to differentiate between shame and remorse. It is patently obvious that there can be shame-motivated suicide without even a hint of remorse; the suicides of Hitler, Goebbels, Himmler and others, especially those in the Nazi hierarchy, at the close of the European War in 1945 exemplifies such an attitude. Death at their own hands was preferable to the humiliation of a public' trial and subsequent execution. (Hitler's Last Will and Testament clearly shows how unrepentant he was about his policies, aggression and mass murder. Similarly, hara-kiri (literally, belly-slitting) sometimes more politely termed seppuku was considered particularly by officers – to be incumbent on the true Japanese warrior if he had failed in his duty (see Carlton: 2002). It was almost as though suicide could compensate for an unavoidable defeat or a believed dereliction of duty, On the other hand, remorse-motivated suicide, as we shall see, is pre-eminently characteristic of a person who has killed someone whom they really cared about, perhaps inadvertently or in a fit of barely controlled rage. It is this kind of crime with which we will now be mainly concerned.

In a classic study which must now unfortunately be considered out of date, Dr. D.J. West, then Assistant Director of Research at The Cambridge Institute of Criminology, presented some questionable statistics on cases of murder followed by suicide (1965). In round figures, he gives the yearly average number of suicides in England

and Wales as 5,000 and the number of murders as 150, of which about a third are followed by suicide. About half of the murders too have been committed by women (often of children) are followed by suicide. It would appear from even earlier figures that the proportion of murderers who commit suicide as remained fairly constant over the years, certainly since the 1920s for which statistics are available. However, the figures for attempted suicides following murder are unclear simply because it is not always certain when such attempts have been made, or indeed whether such attempts were genuine. (Some figures show about suicide generally that although more women than men attempt suicide, more men than women actually succeed). In very general terms, Dr. West concludes that about half the murders in England are followed by suicide or attempted suicide.

It is sometimes contended that because a high proportion of those who commit suicide are said to be suffering from some form of depressive illness, it follows that murder too is committed by those in a state of 'insanity' however that is defined. This is an argument that will be taken up again in the last section of our study, but it will suffice to say that as a causal basis for murder in general, this has yet to be substantiated. Similarly the view that suicide is a form of inwardly-directed aggression as opposed to – or alternative to – murder which is an externally-directed act (a view stemming from Freudian. theory) is also without adequate evidential support. Certainly the idea that the typical suicide victim is in fact a frustrated murderer is hardly tenable. What evidence there is about the states of mind of intending suicides suggests that their emotions may run the gammut from anger to hopelessness.

It is therefore highly contentious that murder and suicide are 'opposite types of adjustment' or that they are 'mutual substitutes'. This seems to be an oversimplification, as is the view of Austin Porterfield that 'the secular, especially upper-class, society is more given to suicide, and the depressed folk society is more given to crime' (quoted by Wolfgang: 1966, p.270). As a conclusion it seems about as useful as Carl Schmid's findings in his early study of Minneapolis that male suicide was highest on Tuesdays and lowest on Fridays, whereas in Philadelphia it was highest on Fridays and Saturdays, and lowest on Mondays and Tuesdays – an inverse pattern which the author regards as 'striking' (ibid. p.271).

West cites some comparative material: for example, figures for the number of murders followed by suicide in New South Wales were found to be only slightly less than England and Wales, whereas in

Denmark the figures were certainly higher (over a third of all murders were by women – so much for 'liberation'). The really interesting contrast is (was?) with the USA where it was reported that only four percent of those who commit murder subsequently kill themselves. The overwhelming majority of homicides were by males, and these figures have been confirmed from various American cities.

Where murder/manslaughter followed by suicide occurs, the pattern – pretty well known impressionistically – is that of the killing of a lover or spouse, most commonly the woman. Jealousy combined with intense anger seems to be the most common motive, a factor found also in some homosexual relationships. Suicide following child murder also features prominently in the statistics – a crime which the perpetrators seem to regard as altruistic, but which is certainly based on a distorted view of the parent-child relationship. Sometimes, though rarely, there is a suicide pact. This may involve mutual suicides (such as that of the writer Arthur Koestler and his wife), or an agreement whereby one murders the other and then takes his/her own life (West cites a case where ·a husband, his wife, and his mistress all died together of aspirin and gas poisoning, and it was assumed to be an instance of three suicides). Such arrangements fall into an anomalous category as far as official statistics are concerned as does those rare occurrences where a suicide by gas poisoning has also resulted in the accidental death of someone else in the house. Also rather unusual are the cases where there is a notable delay between the murder/manslaughter and the subsequent suicide. This may, of course, not be occasioned by remorse, but by a dawning realization that the chances of a light sentence or even of an · unproven case look increasingly unlikely.

Murder followed by suicide has been shown to be largely a domestic phenomenon. In one study of 148 offenders, 62 were men who had killed their wives or girlfriends, 52 were women who had killed their children, 15 were men who had killed their children (and in some cases wives as well), and only 3 cases of a woman who had killed a husband or lover. In virtually every instance the tragedy had taken place in the home, and in no case was theft involved. All the child victims were under 16 years of age, and it is perhaps significant that contrary to the view that mothers may kill children during postnatal depression, only 11 of the infants were under a year old. These figures, as we have seen, are rather dated, but they still give a useful general impression, although Home Office statistics from the 1980s suggest that they should be somewhat lower (Leyton: 1997, pp. 235-36). The samples cited had to be selected and not random, but their findings were nevertheless valid indications of overall trends in England and Wales, and in the United States.

Brief consideration of three cases, two typical and one atypical, will serve as examples of the homicide-suicide phenomenon. The first is that of a middle-aged man who had apparently worked satisfactorily for the same firm all his life. Inexplicably, he stole a modest sum of money from the firm and was subsequently detected and told to leave. In view of his long service, he was not prosecuted, and although not in dire straits financially, he became what those who knew him regarded as 'unduly anxious' about his situation even though he knew that his previous employers were not going to take matters any further. A few days later he murdered his wife to whom he had always seemed devoted, and then killed himself.

The second was a particularly sensational case in the USA, so sensational, in fact, that it has been seen fit (or profitable) to serve it up for public consumption as a Hollywood film (Death of a Centrefold). It concerned the murder of Dorothy Stratten (real name, Hoogstratten) an attractive Vancouver waitress who eventually became a model for Playboy magazine. Her 'Svengali', was Paul Snider whom she married and under whose grooming and management her career prospered. But as it did so, and she became more ambitious and independent, he became resentful and jealous. There were serious arguments, partings and temporary reconciliations. Hollywood beckoned and a new world was opening up for her. She asked for a divorce, and he refused. She was only twenty-one, and she wanted her freedom. This was all too much for Snider. On August 14th 1980, he killed her in their bedroom in Los Angeles, and then shot himself with the same gun.

The atypical case (given by Leyton, 1997, p.218) is that of a murderer who committed suicide after his second and more serious crime. The man from South Yorkshire who had already served six years in prison in the 1980s for raping a sixteen year old girl, later assaulted and murdered a twenty-two year old waitress, Sandra Parkinson, as she was out for a walk. The man still only in his thirties – obviously deeply troubled by what he had done, hanged himself from a tree in Cambridgeshire. He left a note for the Parkinson family which said, 'I can't do anything to help you through your grief. All I can do is to kill myself. I hope it helps, even if its just a bit'. There could, of course, be no adequate restitution or compensation. But some will feel that he, at least, did the 'honourable' thing.

As a complementary and rather poignant footnote, it is perhaps worth mentioning an initially baffling case in Singapore. A Japanese couple were found dead in what appeared to be an open and shut case. The body of the twenty-nine year old husband was found meticulously laid out with a handkerchief over his face and a blanket over his body. His wife was found with her ankles tied hanging from a roof beam. The immediate impression was that the husband, a schoolteacher, had hanged his wife – possibly after a serious quarrel – and then committed suicide. But on further investigation it was discovered that this was a kind of Romeo and Juliet scenario. The husband had not committed suicide but had suffered a sudden, massive heart attack. His wife – Atsumi – on discovering the body, had decided to join him by taking her own life. It was a ritual that is followed very rarely by modern Japanese. But in this case, Atsumi – tragically, many would feel was an old-fashioned girl.

iv) MURDER AND SEXUAL GRATIFICATION

Tennyson Jesse once hazarded the hypothesis that there was a strange and inexplicable affinity between murderers and their victims. She suggested that to the impartial onlooker it was almost like the attitude of a bird to a snake. She suggested, very speculatively, that possibly at some future date when the laws of attraction and repulsion are more fully understood it may be discovered that this affinity has a kind of extrasensory (in her terms 'wavelength') dimension. This highly conjectural idea has its roots in Freud's death-wish (Thanatos) theory. But it is a far cry from maintaining that we all have an instinct for wishing our own demise, and of resignedly anticipating that demise.

This kind of theory – inasfar as it has any applicability at all – is sometimes advanced in relation to murders for sexual gratification. Where the case is not that of a stranger killing (as so many serial rape/murder cases are) the idea may have a very limited cogency (but may apply where women – unaccountably – are attracted to convicted killers). But beyond this, it would appear to be an experiential non-starter. It is true that some young women, for example, are attracted to the wrong kind of man, and eventually become their victims, as in such classic cases as that of Henri Landru (the French 'Bluebeard'), Henri de Tourville, and George Joseph Smith, the notorious 'Brides-in-the-Bath' murderer.

But in these and many other 'Love from a.Stranger' cases the real motive was. greed rather than sex. Killers like Peter Sutcliffe (the 'Yorkshire Ripper') hardly come into this category. Neither does it apply to such people as Richard Ramirez, the serial killer known as the 'Night Stalker' who comes very close to the kind of person with whom we are particularly concerned in this section of our discussion. Ramirez terrorised the Los Angeles and San Francisco areas in 1985 committing various felonies including burglary, rape and murder. His customary modus operandi was to enter houses at night, raping and killing his female victims after first having disposed of any inconvenient males. Some victims survived these assaults, and described their assailant as a young man dressed in black, with a gaunt face and discoloured teeth who made frequent references to the devil. Before long he became careless, and his orange coloured car was spotted, classified and found abandoned. He already had a police record, and was therefore quickly identified. A photograph of the twenty-five year old appeared in the newspapers, and he was eventually cornered after being chased by an irate crowd in the street.

For reasons which are hardly explicable to those used to British court procedures, he was tried -four years later and sentenced to death on thirteen counts of murder and thirty other felonies. He told the judge at his trial that he should be shown no mercy because he was 'beyond good and evil'.

Perhaps he was sincere. But it is notable that when the detectives who interrogated him asked him why he had embarked upon such an horrific spree of rape and murder, he simply replied, 'Because I like to kill people'. Criminals often make all sorts of feeble excuses to explain their behaviour – excuses which they may even come to believe themselves. But when they admit killing simply because they like it, we have reached the reductionist ne plus ultra.

This is not to suggest that there is no such thing as a genuinely disturbed individual – a murderer who is so mentally unbalanced that his crimes defy explanation. What are we to make, for example, of Gary Heidnik who kept women captive in a dilapidated house in Philadelphia so that he could torture and rape them at will? His crimes only came to light in 1987 when a woman who had escaped claimed that she had been held prisoner for four months in the basement where she and others had been systematically abused. When police raided the house they found it as the woman had described with the ominous addition of a refrigerator containing human remains. The woman further insisted that they had been fed on dog food mixed with minced human flesh. From their investigations the police concluded that at least two girls had been murdered there – though maybe many more. Obviously they were seen as disposable once Heidnik had tired of them. In which case he would cruise the streets in his expensive Cadillac, respectably attired, looking for fresh victims.

Heidnik is said to have had a classic serial killer's biography. He came from a broken home where he was often beaten by a racist, alcoholic father (One could so easily become cynical here and ask where was the negligent prostitute mother to complete the picture? So many youngsters start with similar disadvantages, yet certainly don't turn out as 'strange' as Heidnik). Though not unintelligent he did badly at school. He was admitted to the Army, but by 1968 he was showing suspicious signs of mental instability and was diagnosed as a schizophrenic and discharged with a hundred per cent disability pension.

It transpired that Heidnik had been periodically admitted to psychiatric units since his discharge during which time he had attempted suicide several times. In 1978 he was sent to prison for sexually assaulting a mentally retarded women. But when he was paroled in 1983 his own mental condition did not prevent him from playing the stock market from which he made a small fortune. (At the time of his trial, he still had about $300,000, and could therefore afford expensive legal representation). With the money he embarked on yet a · further uncharacteristic venture; he founded a religious organisation of which he claimed to be the bishop. Meetings were held at his home, but complaints were soon made about the rock music which he had introduced as part of the rituals.

His bizarre behaviour was not taken into consideration as possible mitigation for his crimes. He was found guilty on two counts of murder and four of rape, and sentenced to death. It was reported that his father was so disgusted and -disillusioned about the whole affair that he said he would gladly act as executioner.

It could well be argued that in Heidnik's case there was significant evidence of mental disturbance before he actually embarked on his worst crimes. There had obviously been a build-up of strange behaviour patterns. The tell-tale indications were there. Though few – if any – could have foretold that they would culminate in such horrible excesses. But what of the individual who has led an apparently blameless life who then – seemingly without provocation – suddenly embarks on a short but terrible killing spree? Such was the case with Gordon Cummins.

In February 1942, a girl was found strangled in an air-raid shelter in Marylebone. On the following night another girl was found strangled in her Soho flat. She was a former Windmill Girl – obviously not averse to displaying her charms – who was now presumably working as a prostitute. All that could be deduced from the crime scene and the mutilations on her body was that the murderer was almost certainly left-handed. Only four days later, a third victim was discovered, similarly strangled and mutilated, in a flat in Tottenham Court Road: The toll was becoming truly frightening when within a few hours, a fourth victim was found in similar circumstances in the Paddington area.

The police had enough to do in wartime London, but in this case their task was made easy by the inexplicable carelessness of the killer. In his frantic obsession he had also riskily attacked a woman in a darkened doorway not far from Piccadilly. He was disturbed by passers-by, and in his haste dropped his service respirator which gave police his name and number. Gordon Cummins, a married man, was quickly traced to his billet in North London and duly charged with the murders.

Cummins, an educated man who tended to parade his knowledge among his fellow servicemen, was tried at the Old Bailey in April. The forensic evidence was conclusive and he was found guilty and executed two months later. (The Old British justice system knew nothing of the never ending appeals procedures that characterize so many American courts). But how it all began and what precipitated it, no one was ever quite sure.

Uncertainty also surrounds a similar series of murders also in London. The crimes were so reminiscent of the six 'Jack the Ripper' killings which took place within the space of three months in Whitechapel in 1888, for which no one was ever convicted, that the media dubbed these the 'Jack the Stripper' murders. The first body was found on the bank of the Thames not far from Hammersmith Bridge one dark morning in February 1964. From the position of the body, the police estimated that it had been dumped upstream some twenty-four hours earlier. This would place the murder somewhere near a popular courting area also frequented by prostitutes and was known as Dukes Meadow, and was near Chiswick. The victim was soon identified as an ageing known prostitute who normally plied her trade in the Bayswater Road, and who was pregnant with her third child. She was only five feet two inches (a factor which was later to prove of some significance). Her body was naked except for some cloth stuffed in her mouth and her clothes and her handbag were missing. Curiously, it was difficult to establish exactly how she had died, but tests suggested that besides suffering head injuries, she may have been drowned before being thrown in the river.

Two months later, another body was found in very similar circumstances. Again Dukes Meadow was implicated, and again the victim was a prostitute – only five feet tall- and also pregnant. It was discovered that she had originally featured in pornographic films, but until her death had also worked the Bayswater Road area. In this instance there was no doubt about the cause of death – she had been strangled.

Shortly afterwards, the body of a third prostitute was found, this time in an alleyway in Brentford. By this time the police were becoming understandably alarmed, and top level investigators were allocated to the case. They established that the third victim had originally come from Scotland, had worked as a stripper and had gravitated to Soho where she had mixed with pretty seedy company. From there it was a very short step to prostitution. Examination of the body was made so much easier because it had not been in the water. Forensic examination showed that she had performed fellatio before being strangled and – as a bizarre and inexplicable twist – her front teeth had been forced out after death. The most interesting clue was the presence of tiny flecks of paint on the body which indicated that possibly it had been hidden temporarily in a paint shop where high pressure sprays were used.

As the enquiries were continuing, a middle-aged man came forward and confessed to the second murder. Kenneth Archibald, the owner of a drinking club, was charged, but at the Old Bailey trial he retracted his confession saying that it was all a mistake, and that he was drunk at the time. The jury took only an hour to acquit him, a verdict which seemed to be corroborated by the fact that he had watertight alibis for the other two murders.

The police re-doubled their efforts and searched their files for any record of similar unsolved crimes. They found two: one of a murdered woman" who was found on a towpath near Chiswick in 1959, and another of a woman found in a shallow grave at Mortlake in 1963. If these were indeed victims of the same killer, we are presented with an intriguing instance of periodicity quite unlike that of Gordon Cummins. Instead of an apparently insane haste in seeking victims, here we have significant gaps in the murderer's programme. These are as much in need of explanation as the murder spree phenomenon. And why the increasing incidence of murder with the passage of time? Are we to assume – as some psychiatrists are prone to do – that there is a build-up in the compulsion to mutilate and kill that can no longer be resisted?

The Mortlake grave was painstakingly sifted for any remnants that might reveal even the faintest clue. The victim – or 'Pink Slip Girl', as she was dubbed by the press – once identified, had been known by many more names at different times. There was still little to go on, but her grave did contain a small sliver of flesh on which there was a fingerprint. But it still wasn't enough.

The fifth victim, yet another young woman from the provinces seeking a more exciting life in the metropolis, had been unceremoniously dumped outside a lock-up garage in Chiswick. The man who found it thought at first that it was a discarded tailor's dummy. She too was a prostitute working the Bayswater Road area, and she too had swallowed sperm and had her front teeth removed after death.

She also had minute spots of paint on her, so although it was obvious that the killer was keeping to his usual stamping ground, the police still could not determine where the bodies were being hidden.

The killer was getting bolder. Victim number six was found in a car park just off Kensington High Street. It was soon discovered that she was already known to the police because she had once given evidence in the Stephen Ward case, after which Ward had committed suicide. Ward had been accused of procuring girls, notably Christine Keeler and Mandy Rice Davies, for well-known personalities, most notably John Profumo, then a government minister. The police, however, were convinced that these high-profile goings-on had nothing to do with the latest murder.

In February 1965, just a year after the case had come to the police's attention, a further body was found, again in an alley. The victim was another prostitute whose body had certainly been kept somewhere for a month before it was discovered near a railway line. The police received yet further reinforcements until eventually over three hundred officers were involved besides top detectives from Scotland Yard. London became literally saturated with police. Records were checked and re-checked;. women officers dressed as prostitutes and spoke to. working girls and their clients. Then came a crackdown on vice, with officers promising leniency in exchange for cooperation and information. Certain traffic movements were logged; clients and kerb-crawlers were rounded up and grilled about their activities at the relevant times – but still nothing.

Finally, the cross-referencing of this mountain of data began to produce results. The police located the dilapidated paint shop they had been looking for, and detectives gradually narrowed the search to three men, and then to just one. He was a married man who lived in

South London and who worked as a security guard. The man took his own life before he could be charged, so technically the murders have still not been solved. But the man who was never officially named left a note which was tantamount to a confession and the crimes ceased with his death. The question remains: if those who commit crimes like these are to be considered abnormal (and statistically – if for no other reason such a conclusion is unavoidable) can this in any way excuse their crimes? Does it minimize their guilt? If it is thought to do so, then are we not saying, in effect, that the more horrendous the crime, the lighter the sentence?

Tragically, cases of this kind are far from rare. Murder for sexual gratification often combined with various sadistic trimmings are all too common especially with serial killers. Melvin Rees killed at least five people, and probably more, in Maryland and Virginia between 1957 and 1959. He became known as the 'Sex Beast' and was convicted and electrocuted in 1961. John Collins, a twenty-two year old student, was found responsible for the so-called 'Co-ed Murders' which were committed between 1967 and 1969. Seven co-eds were killed in the Ypsilanti area of Michigan, and at first the police were so baffled that they called in the services of 'psychic detective' Peter Hurkos. This proved to be a fruitless exercise, as it so often had in other puzzling cases (see Carlton 2000). These young girl students had been either strangled or shot, as well as being mutilated. Collins was found guilty on the basis of convincing forensic evidence and sentenced to life imprisonment. Another very similar case is that of thirty-four year old Richard Cottingham described as a computer expert, who killed at least fifteen prostitutes in New Jersey and New York City between 1977 and 1980. Cottingham, a family man, regarded prostitutes as a class of women who should be punished, and he subjected them to rape and torture before they were killed. The law made sure that he would never be free to repeat such crimes; in all his prison sentences totalled 250 years.

Serial murder has not, of course, been confined to women. The homosexual murders of Dennis Nilsen in London were more than matched by those of John Wayne Gacey in Chicago, and those of Dean Corll in Houston, Texas who preceded him. Corll's infamous career began in 1973, and his killings came to light when he, in turn, was killed by teenage accomplice, Elmer Henley who – so he claimed – believed that Corll was all set to kill him. Henley and another accomplice acted as procurers for Corll who, like Gacey, was an outwardly respected citizen, but was also a sexual sadist. It is estimated that he assaulted and killed upwards of twenty-seven boys between 1973 and 1974, their bodies being concealed either in a boat-shed or in woodland. (Parents apparently believed they had absconded to join some hippie movement or another). Henley for his part in the crimes was sentenced to 594 years in prison, and another teenage accomplice was given a life sentence.

More recently the UK has seen the conviction of David Mulcahy for his part in a series of rapes and murders going back to 1982. With his boyhood friend John Duffy he stalked the North London parklands and railway stations looking for possible victims. The pair had been misfits at school, truanting and avoiding study and particularly Exams. Both had a series of menial jobs, but compensated by the excitement of carrying out innumerable rapes and sexual assaults (nobody seems to know quite how many) about which they had originally only fantasized. These degenerated into murder in 1985, and between then and 1988 when Duffy was arrested, there were three known victims. Duffy had always promised never to betray his accomplice – a vow he kept for nine years. Mulcahy judiciously never visited his friend in prison or tried to contact him. Neither did he arrange to disappear. When he was arrested in 1999, he tried to bluff it out, and once in court protested that Duffy was a liar. But the evidence was overwhelming. Both men are now serving life sentences, and it is doubtful if either will ever be released.

Monsters of this kind are almost impossible to fathom. Most crimes – even 'run-of-the-mill' murder – are not that difficult to understand, but sadism and the actual enjoyment of murder is a thing apart. What we can say is that such people have no place in what we like to call a civilized society.

EXCURSUS: SEX CRIME AND SEXUAL DYSFUNCTION

A few years ago at a National Sex Forum Symposium held in San Francisco, its Director maintained that male sexual dysfunction was the 'primary sex problem of modern society', and further hypothesized that sex crime and violence were expressions of a 'warped mentality' which derived from this condition.

This is a view to which not everyone would subscribe, but it does reflect a suspicion that some sex crime is not the result of rampant bestiality but a desire by dysfunctional males to dominate their victims. Indeed, some theorists would go further and argue that 'women's liberation' has generated a culture of female assertiveness and expectation which many males have found intimidating. Hence the increasing incidence of sexual assault, almost as a form of revenge. The sex attack sometimes accompanied by killing (as in the case of multiple murderer, Reginald Christie), thus becomes a kind of male counter-assertion possibly by men who cannot easily function under normal circumstances.

It is pertinent, then, to ask whether male sexual dysfunction is really on the increase (the term dysfunction is here preferred to impotence which implies a pervasive condition; a person may be dysfunctional only in particular sets of circumstances). Anecdotal evidence, advice column enquiries, popular articles (especially in women's magazines), and certainly the work of sex therapists, all suggest that sexual dysfunction is a real problem. There is, of course, a great deal of pseudo-psychology on offer, as well as tit-bits to stimulate the Sunday morning palate. But whatever form it takes, there is a growing concern. Perhaps too much is expected of the modern male, and this may have given rise to a deep uncertainty. Men are tempted to ask 'Can it happen to me?', and nothing that is written or said can leave them with iron-clad guarantees.

So what are the most common reasons given for sexual dysfunction? And what theories are regarded as plausible? At best. we can say that a number of general explanations have been given, although in any particular case, dysfunction may be related to anyone or combination of the following:

i) dysfunction has a purely physical basis. Therapists are divided on this issue. Most appear only to attribute sexual dysfunction to hormonal imbalance, post-operative surgery, obesity, drugs, etc. in a minority of cases. Others (e.g. Martin Cole) have argued that eventually we will discover that as much as 60 per cent of male dysfunction has some physical basis. (N.B. that certain drugs prescribed for such conditions as diabetes, blood pressure, etc. may have deleterious effects on sexual performance). Hence the arrival of Viagra.

ii) dysfunction is really a state of mind. Psychologists also vary on this point. It may be due to problems of learning, guilt and repression. Failure may then generate a fear syndrome. Ignorance may also be a factor which, in turn, is related to incorrect or inadequate sex education (But note the contrary view that it is 'knowledge' that leads to dysfunction. Do we all know too much? see (v).

iii) dysfunction derives from one's social situation. Business anxieties, money worries, frustrating work routines etc. Sexual failure is seen to be the possible result of the attendant pressures of a competitive society – especially in middle-age.

iv) dysfunction is a response to increased feminine demands. Part of the women's liberation thesis is that women are becoming more aware of their own sexual potential. So do these heightened expectations produce a fear of women, and result in consequent male sexual inhibitions?

v) dysfunction results from unrealistic 'performance' standards. Critics ask, what is normal? What ought people's sex expectations to be? Is there a tendency in modern society towards the mechanization of sex, and thus to an over-emphasis on sexual athleticism

Whether male sexual dysfunction can be related particularly to the hypothesized imperatives of women's liberation is debatable. But there is certainly a wider range of normative expectations reflected in what some regard as the 'new' sexual permissiveness. Psychological responses may therefore be largely induced, thus producing a sense of sexual alienation in the male. For certain kinds of personality it may-then be quite a short step to displays of otherwise inexplicable violence. This is not to excuse or rationalise that violence, but simply explain and understand it.

v) MURDER AND JEALOUSY

It is well known that extreme jealousy can sometimes lead to sudden, provoked acts of violence. And, as we shall see, murder can result from that prolonged, knawing sense of anger and humiliation which is also generated by jealousy. In the first set of circumstances, the violence is usually unpremeditated, and may afterwards be the cause of extreme anguish and regret. Whereas in the second set of circumstances the result may be an act of carefully calculated revenge.

There are, however, cases which do not fall neatly into either category, namely those in which a prolonged, corrosive situation finally culminates in an explosion of violence. Such was the case of Florence Ransome a thirty-five year old widow charged with triple murder in Matfield, Kent in July 1940. It all happened at a time when England, and particularly the Southern Counties were beginning to experience the first phase of the German bombing campaign which preceded the Blitz that followed in September. The first and most strategically rational phase of the Luftwaffe air offensive concentrated on the southern airfields, just the area where the murders took place. In retrospect it seems commonsense that in these times people would have more to worry about than the violent resolution of domestic triangles.

Florence Ransome was the mistress of Walter Fisher with whom she had been living at a farm in Oxfordshire. His wife, Dorothy, and grown-up daughter Freda, still lived at the family home in Matfield. One assumes that they had accepted the situation because it is known that Walter Fisher often visited them there in the company of Mrs Ransome. But it is equally clear that this was not the case with Mrs Ransome. On the fatal day, she travelled from Oxfordshire to Kent where she was expected for tea, carrying (as observers later testified) a single barrelled shot gun – showing every evidence of premeditation. On arriving at Matfield, she shot both Dorothy Fisher and her daughter as well as their maid, an inconvenient witness to the first two murders. But having retrieved the three spent cartridges, in her haste she left behind an incriminating glove. She was quickly apprehended, and at her trial at the Old Bailey pleaded 'Not Guilty' in the face of irrefutable evidence. The jury deliberated for less than an hour, and Florence Ransome who had a history of mental instability, was found guilty and committed to Broadmoor Asylum for the criminally insane.

A rather similar case in recent years among the 'White Mischief' set of post-colonial Africa is that of fifty year old Marietta Bosch who was convicted of killing her lover's wife in Botswana. Rita Wolmarans was shot twice in the head in June 1996 by a woman who was said to be her best friend, but who wanted to marry her husband with whom she had been having an affair for several months. Initially, suspicion had fallen upon the husband. but there was no clear evidence to charge him either with the murder of even of complicity. Marietta Bosch's husband had been killed in a car crash only five months before her affair with Tienie Wolmarans had begun. Her lover had apparently promised to divorce his wife in order to marry her, but it was part of the prosecution's case that she could not wait (or perhaps secretly believed that the divorce was never going to happen) and therefore decided to kill the woman who stood between her and her lover. In the circumstances, it was not just a crime it was an impatient blunder.

Three months after the murder, the couple were quietly engaged, and when Marietta Bosch was finally arrested, they married while she was out on bail. The case against her was admittedly circumstantial, but the prosecution case was quite convincing despite the lack of supporting evidence.

Jealousy is such a common motive for murder and takes so many different forms that it is instructive to look at further cases in a little more detail. In the annuls of English crime, one of the best known is the Elvira Barney case in 1932. It is well known because it had a -high social profile, and because of the somewhat · surprising outcome at the Old Bailey trial. Mrs Elvira Barney, a twenty-six year old socialite, came from the wealthy Mullens family of stockbrokers, and was separated from her American husband whom she had married three years before. She was one of the much-vaunted 'bright young things' who frequented the London clubs at a time when much of the country was in deep recession. Some described her as attractive, but she was in fact somewhat overweight, not particularly what in those days would have been regarded as 'refined', and was not unusually the worse for wear. At the time of the crime she was living with Scott Stephen, two years her junior, who vaguely referred to himself as a dress designer. Given that he had no fixed abode nor any visible means of support he had battened on to this rather coarse but well-heeled woman as a convenient if temporary meal-ticket.

The murder took place in May 1932 in a mews maisonette off Lowndes Square in London at four in the morning. Elvira Barney shot and killed Stephen during a furious argument possibly fuelled by drink. It was by no means the first quarrel they'd had, nor was it the first time that Mrs Barney had threatened to shoot her lover. (Indeed, police later found a bullet hole in the wall which – she admitted – was the result of an earlier attempt to 'frighten' Stephen). At her trial she insisted that in a jealous rage she had told him to get out, and that she had then taken the revolver – which seems always to have been to hand – with the intention of killing herself. Stephen – so she said – had remonstrated with her and had tried to grab the gun, and that it had gone off in the ensuing struggle and killed him. She had then phoned the doctor babbling incoherently about someone 'bleeding to death'. When the doctor arrived he had found her sobbing hysterically and threatening to kill herself. (It is perhaps worthy of note that when the police arrived at the murder scene and told Mrs Barneyshe was under arrest, she flew into an uncontrollable rage and struck the Inspector whom she called 'a vile swine' and boasted about the social (family) connections).

The police found no sign of struggle in the apartment, and saw no reason to believe they were dealing with anything other than a murder. The eminent pathologist, Sir Bernard Spilsbury, whose testimony as an expert witness had put the rope around more than one neck, confirmed these findings. But the prosecution had to deal with one of the most brilliant barristers of his day, Sir Patrick Hastings, whose services had been secured by the defendant's wealthy parents. On what must now seem to be rather flimsy counter evidence relating to the question of how or in which hand the revolver was held, Hastings was able to convince the jury that the shooting *could have* been accidental. Given therefore that the accused can be given the benefit of the doubt, Elvira Barney who presented a suitably demure picture in court, was found to be not guilty and consequently acquitted.

Having learned few lessons, this unstable and volatile woman returned to her old life, presumably relishing her ill-gotten fame. Within a few years the woman who had shouted to her lover, 'Laugh baby, laugh for the last time', had herself died – possibly as the result of her excesses – in Paris. How she became what she was, 'is anyone's guess. Having so many advantages, she threw them all away for a life of empty sensation-seeking. But then there is still a prevalent trend in our culture – the experiential taking precedence over the rational. (This had certain echoes in the case of Fiona Mont, otherwise known as 'the Cat', who was accused of serious fraud charges. Her parents gave her an expensive education, and were held responsible by the press for her behaviour because they were too 'rigid and disciplinarian'. Is that really *so* bad?)

Popular crime writer, Rupert Furneaux, once observed – perhaps with some exaggeration – that more lethal bullets are fired in the United States in a day than in Britain in a decade. But he concedes that the British are fast catching up. He adds that when the British housewife or deceived mistress reaches for a weapon, her hand seldom alights on anything more destructive than a piece of crockery, whereas in the USA firearms seem to lurk in every woman's bottom drawer. This is, of course, more than slightly tongue-in-cheek, and is certainly not a response that is confined to women. Jealousy knows nothing about gender, although our next two cases are concerned with women who 'have resorted to murder.

Frank Young (or Caesar Young, as he was often called) was a well-known high-rolling gambler who was shot in a cab on Broadway after a somewhat hectic night out on the town. The driver who appears to have been in a similarly befuddled state, drew up sharply, and saw the dying man draped across the lap of his other passenger, an attractive girl who was fruitlessly crying, 'Caesar, why did you do this?' Her tears seemed as genuine as her concern. Suicide albeit under rather strange circumstances – seemed to be corroborated by the recently fired.32 revolver found in the man's pocket. But it was the wrong pocket for a right-handed man. And how many alcohol-confused suicides would have been thoughtful enough to shoot themselves and then put the gun away afterwards?

The police investigation revealed that Frank Young was on the point of leaving his lady friend, the passenger Nan Patterson, and was due to sail for Europe with his wife later that morning. Nan Patterson was a showgirl who had been his mistress for the better part of two years, and it became known that they'd had a furious argument the night before in which he had hit her and sworn never to see her again, and that she had retaliated with ill-defined threats, even hinting that her paramour would never make the trip.

So was this suicide or murder? It transpired that the revolver had been recently purchased by Nan Patterson's brother. The police had no doubts, and Patterson was indicted on a charge of murder. The media had no doubts either, and had effectively tried the case before the trial had begun. The prosecution, however, were not so sure – not about Patterson's guilt, 'but whether they could secure a conviction of an attractive woman with an all-male jury. Her defence lawyer, Abe Levy, a veteran of some three hundred homicide cases, dismissed the prosecution's talk of powder burns and bullet trajectories as so much confabulation. He insisted that the interpretation of events was simple: Young had repented of his harsh treatment of his mistress, implored her forgiveness, and when she refused had shot himself in a fit of drunken despair. He went further. In a hearts-and-flowers appeal, he asked the jury how they could possibly believe that this – albeit – frivolous, pleasure-loving girl 'could conceive such a murderous plot and then try to obfuscate the issue with 'subtle invention'? This should require the ingenuity of a consummate actress not the ingenuousness of a showgirl.

This was not the first trial. The original trial was aborted when a juror suddenly died. This second trial in which District Attorney Rand and defence lawyer Levy had fought to a stalemate ended in deadlock when the jury failed to agree on a verdict. The third trial jury were almost unanimous on Patterson's guilt – but not quite because just one juror would not go along with the rest. He said he 'felt sorry for Nan' – a judgement which had little to do with the evidence. After this the state gave up and withdrew the charge, although it is doubtful whether they were unduly impressed by Mr Levy's argument that Miss Patterson was 'too exhausted' to stand yet a further trial.

The public, who had followed the case avidly, seemed in general to be pleased with the outcome, though few can have doubted that she had impulsively done away with a valuable 'rich uncle'.

Nan Patterson whom the newspapers had once confidently predicted would 'fry', now became a celebrity. She had previously been a modest member of the chorus of Floradora but now went on to scale new heights in her theatrical career, and was soon reputedly earning $1,000 a week in a show called The Lulu Girls. Soon afterwards she was remarried to a husband that she had once obscurely divorced, and from thence passed into the overcrowded realms of American legend.

M. Marc Ancel, Judge of the Supreme Court of France, gave it as his opinion in 1956 that attitudes were changing concerning the crime of passion. He said that whereas in the past French juries had taken a lenient view of killings alleged to have been done out of jealousy, since 1945 when women were admitted as jurors.a less sympathetic view seemed to be prevalent. Consequently in 1951 when Pauline Dubuisson was charged with having shot her lover, Felix Bailey, a young medical student in what appeared to be a fit of jealousy a more open-minded view is assumed to have. existed. The couple were found together in a gas-filled room: he was dead, an automatic was lying on the floor, and she was pretty far gone and had to be revived with oxygen. It looked like a straightforward case, until the police examined the body. Bailey had been shot three times, twice in the forehead. and once through the back of the neck, not quite the 'format' that one would expect in a lovers' quarrel. Indeed, the more they looked into things, the more this appeared to be a capital crime. Bailey's death began to look like a clinically calculated killing.

When detectives searched Dubuisson's room they found her diary (described at her trial as the 'Orgy Book') which clearly showed that she was not the beautiful innocent that she appeared. Her love affairs had begun at the age of fourteen with a German soldier during the Occupation. She had then graduated to nude parties with German officers, and had been expelled from school for recounting the details (or boasting about them) too often to her classmates. To escape deportation for forced labour in Germany – the fate of so many young non-Jewish people in the occupied territories – she had acquired a 'protector', a Nazi doctor who regarded her, in her own words, as a 'tasty mistress'. It was the kind of reputation that would not go down at all well with a French jury who would see her as a collaborating whore who was fortunate not to have been shot by the Resistance. However, she was able to evade the recriminations and revenge of people at the end of hostilities and escape to Lyons. There she enlisted as a medical student and eventually did well in her training and in her Exams.

It was in medical school where she is said to have had the pick of the male students that she met Felix Bailey. Her popularity ensured that she could trifle with his affections just as she pleased. She made no secret of her other affairs, and appears to have delighted in taunting him at times with stories of her other lovers. Eventually, it all became too much for him and he left for Paris where he met another girl to whom he subsequently became engaged. When Pauline Dubuisson heard of this she regarded it as a form of humiliation. This is what she did to others, not what was done to her. So she made a bid to get him back by faking her own suicide – a stratagem which still drew no response. When this did not work, according to the Public Prosecutor, she went to Paris and killed him.

Once in prison she again attempted suicide, this time by cutting her wrists, and the trial was delayed until she had recovered. Finally, the trial. took place in November 1953. Her defence attorney tried to depict her as a much abused, rather pathetic creature – a victim of wartime conditions (and she apparently did present a rather sweet, innocent figure in court). But her diary showed otherwise. The prosecution saw her as a depraved creature who had betrayed her people, her lover and – in a sense – herself, and demanded the death sentence. She admitted her guilt and owned that in a mood of obsessive jealousy she had obtained the gun for the express purpose of killing her ex-lover. There had been no struggle. She had shot him, and to make sure he was dead she had deliberately fired an extra bullet into the back of his neck.

The jury of six men and one woman had no doubts about the verdict. But they had about the sentence. Death was normally mandatory for premeditated murder, yet they obviously could not condemn this now rather pathetic young women to the guillotine. Instead she was sentenced to life imprisonment. It may not have been a popular decision nor even a just one. But in the circumstances, for Mlle. Dubuisson, it was certainly a fortunate one. It would appear that on so grave a charge, and with her wartime reputation, the verdict might well have been otherwise. She had obviously been one of those very knowing teenagers who was able to trade her physical charms for a comfortable life during the Occupation while most other people were keeping their heads down and getting by as best as they could. Her kind of collaboration was despised by most, but it was now eight years after the war and memories had dimmed a little, and possibly her sexuality was still able to exert its magic.

vi) MURDER, MAYHEM AND CULTISM

Some crimes are difficult to fathom because there seems to be no discernible motive such as those of Beverley Allit a twenty-three year old nurse who was convicted of murdering four babies in 1993. She was also almost certainly responsible for the severe illnesses of many others, possibly by giving them high doses of insulin (see also the Kenneth Barlow case). The motive was assumed to be Munchausen's Syndrome by Proxy, a condition in which people are said to gain attention from the illness of others. Whether such a 'Syndrome' has any objective reality, or whether it is simply a term used to describe or interpret a certain kind of behaviour is a moot point. One is bound to wonder if like some other murders of a similar kind it was more of a 'playing god' activity.

The Allit case was not unlike that of Richard Angelo; a male nurse in New York State who 'earned' the sobriquet 'Angel of Death' in 1987. He was thought to be responsible for ten to twenty murders by injecting patients with Pavulon to modify their 'medical destiny'. Earlier still, another nurse in San Antonio, Texas was convicted of the murder of certain infants in her care, and was believed to have been implicated in the deaths of many more. Genene Jones used succinylcholine, a muscle relaxant, rather too freely, and in 1982 was given two concurrent sentences, one of 99 years and another of 60 years. The much more recent case of Dr Harold Shipman may fall into the same category except that his victims, probably numbering at least 150, were elderly people. So far, attempted fraud has only been established in the case of the last victim. Other than this, the motive for murder remains elusive.

If in such cases the motive is not easily discerned, in other cases, it remains incomprehensible. That is to say the crimes or acts that accompany the crimes, are so bizarre as to defy normal conventions. For instance, 'ritual acts' such as cannibalism, as was seen in the crimes of Jeffrey Dahmer in Milwaukee between 1978 and 1991. He was sentenced to life imprisonment for fifteen murders, and to no one's distress was clubbed to death by fellow prisoners in 1994. Similarly with Arthur Shawcross, a serial killer with a full repertoire of perversions who learned his 'trade' in Vietnam, and who killed two children in 1972. For this he was incomprehensibly given only a twenty-five year sentence (of which he then only served fifteen years), and went on to kill eleven prostitutes after his release in 1987. These and possibly other murders were committed between 1988 and 1989, and he was given a ludicrous 250 year sentence. This is typically the kind of case which begs the question squarely faced by Senator Bush in Texas as to why such creatures should be allowed to live.

Equally difficult to explain is the so-called cult murder. Reasons of a kind are usually forthcoming, but how convincing and persuasive are they? One of the classic examples in modern times was the Manson-inspired 'Helter Skelter' killings of actress Sharon Tate and others in August 1969, together with the La Bianca murders two days later. These can be seen as quasi-revolutionary acts; as senseless attempts to precipitate some form of social upheaval. Certainly there was a kind of 'us-and-them' component to the killings; the violent reaction of the dispossessed against those who represented the dominant capitalist culture. What, however, is particularly interesting about the Manson case is how this alienated, ex-criminal and would-be popular musician was able to recruit a 'Family' of young people who were not only attracted to a 'liberated' sex and drugs lifestyle, but who were also susceptible to such murderous urges. The crimes of these youthful perpetrators were violent in the extreme. By and large, they had been brought up in respectable middle-class homes and had presumably been exposed to traditional ethical norms, yet they evinced no obvious remorse for what they had done. It was as though they saw murder as its own justification. The victims were 'pigs' who deserved what they got. These attitudes may be seen as the mindless reductio ad absurdum of the Sixties drop-out, drug-oriented, anti-capitalist culture fostered by urban revolutionaries.

There have been other crimes which have been attributed to 'inner voices'. But whether these are 'genuine' in the sense that those who make such claims really believe them, or whether they are entirely spurious and are simply invoked for exculpatory reasons, is often difficult to know. Peter Sutcliffe, the 'Yorkshire Ripper' made claims of this kind, but – understandably – few people took them seriously. Yet if this was all an entire fabrication, it is a problem to know what the real motives for the murders were. Sutcliffe's crimes do not fall into any 'normal' category. So were his murders a strange cult-like activity, or were they a form of horrific game? (It is known, for example, that people will steal almost worthless items not because they want them, but because their accumulation has become an – irrational – end in itself).

By no means all cult crimes are of the lethal variety. Many are simply carefully devised scams to make money. One of the most profitable frauds was uncovered recently in Japan, a country which because of its liberal tax incentives has become the home of some 20,000 religions and cults. Some of these are very much minority movements: 'Life Space' with only 150 members was, until recently, trying to revive a decaying corpse, as was Kaedajuku with only 50 adherents which holds that mummified bodies can be revived. But these fade into insignificance beside the leaders of the neo-Buddhist Myokaku-ji who in 1996 swindled superstitious and guilt-stricken women out of an estimated £115 million. Their ploy was to exploit yet another aspect of death by claiming to be able to exorcise the spirits of aborted foetuses. 'One is left baffled by the gullability of the public. But then anything is possible apparently in a culture that can produce the Ho-No-Hana-Sanpogyo cult which over four years made £500 million by claiming to diagnose spiritual and mental health by an examination of the feet. To have the soles and toes scrutinised and stroked at £600 a time suggests a culture – or segment of a culture, that is too affluent for its own good.

If we assume that a cult is a kind of esoteric sect, then perhaps the most – bizarre cult incident of recent years was the People's Temple Sect tragedy in 1978. Whether one considers this a form of collective suicide or collective murder, or even a mixture of both, is still a matter of debate. Members of the sect which originated in the USA, were led by the self-appointed Reverend Jim Jones to Georgetown, Guyana where a commune was established. Certain irregularities were uncovered by the authorities, and the sect was warned of further investigations which threatened its existence. The cult members who, by and large, were simple, gullible people were 'persuaded' by their leaders to commit suicide by drinking orange juice laced with cyanide. Some 900 or so died, quite needlessly in a holocaust which to observers made absolutely no sense. (It can hardly be compared with the mass suicide of a similar number of Jews at Masada when besieged by the Romans. Their fate would almost certainly have been the arena where they would have been butchered for entertainment).

More recently still we have had the phenomenon of the 'Solar Temple Cult' whose rituals were a mixture of Catholicism and the occult which drew its 600 or so members mainly from the middle-class, well-educated – and preferably well-heeled – stratum of 'mainly European society. Members paid an annual subscription of £100 plus any extra 'goodwill' donations they cared to make. They also had to stand the exhorbitant costs of the ornate regalia which the organization required. The whole affair was a very elaborate fraud which was set up to fleece its devotees of as much money and property as possible. When investigation put its continuing existence in doubt, the result was murder and suicide: four bodies were found in Canada and forty-eight in Switzerland (1994), plus:sixteen more at Vercors in France (1995), and then five more in Canada (1997). An opportune raid on a Solar Temple satellite at Tenerife in 1998 is believed to have forestalled the mass suicide of another thirty-two people. They were mainly Germans whose leader was a German woman psychologist who apparently believed that members could avoid the imminent end of the world by dying and having their spirits transported aloft to another planet by a waiting spacecraft.

More recent still was the Ugandan 'Doomsday cult' whose death toll may actually exceed that of People's Temple cult in Guyana. The number involved is at least 1,000, but several thousands more are said to be missing. In March 2000, Ugandan authorities exhumed the bodies of 150 cult members, mainly women and children, at one of the movement's compounds at the village of Rugazi. This was the site of one of five mass graves following a church inferno which claimed the lives of 530 cult members. This fire' at the cult's HQ at Kanungu was initially thought to be an act of mass suicide until it was established that many of the dead had been strangled and mutilated. Many of the missing may have come from neighbouring countries and are consequently difficult to trace. And it is ominous that relatives who have been searching for them are said to have been killed by cups of poisoned tea.

Further investigation showed that this is not a straightforward case of religious fanaticism. Simple people were being persuaded to part with their possessions. And the theory is that the killings began when members became disillusioned with the apocalyptic predictions of the cult's leaders and threatened to withdraw their support. This would have doomed the movement which had already spent a fortune trying to recruit new members with its prophecies of the end of the world timed for December 31, 1999. The leaders had apparently promised members personal salvation through divine intervention before the final cataclysm took place.

The cult was organized and run by Joseph Kibwetere, a one-time Roman Catholic who had been excommunicated for what were held to be spurious claims to special revelations. In this he was assisted by a former prostitute, the self-styled Sister Credonia Mwerinde with whom Kibwetere, father of sixteen children, later absconded. Kibwetere was known to have a history of severe mental illness, and had only been released from hospital in 1998. How this was not recognized remains something of a puzzle. It was certainly ignored 'by those Ugandan officials who attended his parties and received his gifts. The third member of the leading triumvirate is Father Dominic Kataribaabo, a defrocked pastor, under whose bedroom and garden 155 bodies were found buried. Of the three, however, it would appear that forty-eight year old Sister Credonia was the person with the greatest influence, and it was she who, according to an ex-cult official, laid down the regimen to be followed by cult members.

The daily routine for devotees was rigorous, and a strict code of silence 'was enforced. Everyone was up at sunrise, and after religious instruction followed by a meagre breakfast, they were required to work in the commune's fields until dusk. The leaders, however, were an exception. They ate well, and enjoyed the fruits of other people's labours. Indeed, Sister Credonia's last and sixth husband over twenty years her senior was reported to have said that the only thing she was really interested in was making money and spending it on eating, drinking and clothes. It transpired that she had earlier invested her savings from prostitution in an illicit banana beer venture which failed in' 1988, whereupon she had a convenient vision which resulted indirectly with her association with Kibwetere, an ex-schoolmaster and civil servant. Together they founded the profitable cult for The Restoration of the Ten Commandments in 1990.

The movement was a syncretistic hotch-potch of traditional Catholicism with superstitious chthonic overtones combined with a particular form of adventism which held that only the redeemed would survive the apocalypse to inherit a 'new earth in year one'. It was therefore quite unnecessary for believers to hold on to their possessions (a common component in the teaching of such cults).

Instead, they should give them over to the cult leaders because a life of luxury awaited them in the new age. Understandably this kind of millenialism had some resonance among impoverished people, not least because not that many years ago the country had experienced the ravages of the Idi Amin regime.

But the date of the final denouement had already been revised once and members were beginning to have a sense of unease. And when unease became questioning disillusionment, the leaders acted with ruthless efficiency. At one site members were drugged and poisoned – possibly with communion wine, and then petrol and sulphuric acid were used to create a blazing inferno. Elsewhere members were either strangled or hacked to death. Whether the leaders did all the killing – a seemingly impossible task – or whether they employed their own special militia, is not known for certain. Certainly the killings were ordered by the leadership, and it may even be that some loyal members were encouraged to turn on the dissenters, typically arguing that dissent was the work of Satan (Sister Credonia is even rumoured to have drunk the blood of sacrificed children in order to ward off 'evil').

There may be yet more bodies, the cult is known to have had centres in particularly remote areas, especially in the forests near the Congolese border (Sunday Telegraph April 2 2000). The cult shares certain characteristics with the Mau Mau movement which arose among the Kikuyu people in the white-dominated Kenya of the 1950s. The main difference being that Mau Mau was essentially a racialist (anti-white), anti-colonialist movement which also had a considerable appeal for the unenfranchised., And when political aspiration is wedded to religious fervour, it can be a very heady concoction indeed.

vii) MURDER AND THE FEAR OF EXPOSURE

There are killers who rape, and rapists who kill. Both are commonly found among serial killers and would include such men as Canadian, Paul Bernadino, a serial rapist who with his wife turned to murder in the early 1990s. A very similar case is that of Douglas Clark, the so-called 'Sunset Slayer' who killed six women from Hollywood's Sunset Strip. After being dishonourably discharged from the Air Force, and having been married and divorced, Clark began to give vent to his extreme sexual fantasies. He met a nurse in 1980 who obviously shared his perversions, and who helped him to locate potential victims. Each encouraged the other to even more extreme violence, including decapitation of the victims; as the nurse said to the police, 'Its fun to kill people...'. When convicted, each blamed the other, but in 1983 Clark was sentenced to death, and his accomplice got life.

Equally familiar are the rapists who become killers because of fear of exposure. The overriding motive is sexual, but the victims are. then silenced to prevent identification of the rapist. A fairly typical case would be that of Craig Crimmins, a twenty-one year old stage hand at New York's Metropolitan Opera House. During a concert interval on July 23 1980, he propositioned and then tried to rape a thirty year old violinist, Helen Mintiks. When she resisted, he stripped her and tied her up, and after further struggles he kicked her down a ventilator shaft where she was found dead by detectives. During questioning, Crimmins finally admitted the crime and at his trial was sentenced to twenty years to life.

There is another well attested kind of situation where a person – usually a man – has become involved with two partners, and has resolved matters by the elimination of one or the other. The most common scenario is either that of a husband who wishes to get rid of his wife in order to marry his mistress, or of a husband who wishes to rid himself of a worrisome mistress who may be pregnant and who is quite unknown to the wife. For whatever reason, it is quite simply a case of a man who wants his freedom and intends to dispose of a woman who has become an encumbrance. Such was the now forgotten Florence Dennis case at Prittlewell in Essex many years ago.

The body of young Florrie Dennis, as she was usually known, was found by a farmworker in a ditch adjoining a rutted, muddy field. She had been shot just underneath the brim of the little straw hat she was happy to wear on special occasions, and then her body had been unceremoniously half-hidden in the ditch. The body was soon identified – a grave mistake on the part of the murderer and the police were quickly in touch with the dead girl's sister, a Mrs Ayriss, who ran a small boarding house at Southend. She told the police that her younger sister had been seeing a man in London and had 'got herself into trouble'. This was an unforgiving society, and it was presumed that the pregnant girl was going to stay with her elder sister and her husband as a way of temporarily concealing her condition.

Further questioning, however, revealed that Mrs Ayriss not only knew the name of the man concerned, but had also enjoyed his attentions for many years before her younger sister had arrived on the scene. Needless to say, the transfer of his attentions to the youthful, unattached Florrie had caused some bitterness and a rift between the sisters. So much so, in fact, that in the interview with the police Mrs Ayriss was prepared to name the man James Canham Read, as the murderer. She said she had already warned her sister about him, but her advice had been defiantly ignored. Mrs Ayriss' husband took it upon himself to telegraph James Read, but received only a curt reply saying that he hadn't seen the 'young person' for eighteen months.

It was difficult for the police to know to what extent these accusations were made out of spite, and to what extent this was a genuine lead. Nothing could be lost by an inquiry, and the police decided to have a talk to Read who worked as a book-keeper at the Royal Albert Docks. But on arriving there they were told that Read, who was obviously not a particularly popular person because of his 'superior ways', had not been in to work recently. So the officers made their way to the hardly salubrious Jamaica Road, Stepney where he lived. There they were confronted by the heretofore Mrs Read, a rather drab figure who was patently worn down. by the task of looking after her seven children. Hers was undoubtedly a failed marriage. She deeply resented her husband whose sartorial extravagances meant that she and the children were left to survive on a mere third of his income. She didn't know that her husband had not been seen at the Docks for several days, and all she could do was to tell the police that they might get more information from the missing man's brother, Harry Read.

It subsequently transpired that not only was James Read missing, but so also was the cash from the cash box in the book-keeper's office. It now seemed pretty obvious that he had panicked after receiving the telegram, taken as much money as he could lay his hands on, and made a sharp exit. But where was he? Appeals went out to the public, newspapers were alerted, but the police had no joy until an inquisitive office boy at the Docks informed them that Read sometimes received letters from Sheerness on the Isle of Sheppey. Furthermore the police discovered that Read had used a post office at Sheerness in earlier days when he was carrying on his somewhat furtive affair with Mrs Ayriss. So why not also with her younger sister?

This was their most promising lead. They found that Read had been conducting a correspondence with Florrie as a Miss Talbot via a shop in Sheerness, while she had been addressing her letters to a Mr Johnson at a shop in Clapham. Read had obviously read an espionage book or two. Further investigation uncovered a telegram sent by Read to Florrie to meet him on the day before the murder. But still Read's whereabouts eluded them.

Weeks went by. Then the police switched their attention to brother Harry on the assumption that their man might get in touch with his brother if he was running short of funds. This simple insight was rewarded. Harry Read received a letter-card with the relevant instructions. But he was cautious and for a time his movements betrayed nothing significant. Then he made a journey to Mitcham in Surrey where at a modest little dwelling known as Rose Cottage the police finally caught up with their man who tried to protest that his name was Thompson. He was arrested and tried at Chelmsford and found guilty of the murder of Florence Dennis for which he was duly hanged. Harry Read, perhaps because he felt in some way complicit, killed himself by walking into a river.

The irony was that poor Florrie had effectively signed her own death warrant with a simple little lie. She had told Read that no one else knew about her pregnancy, so he consequently thought he was safe. But in fact she had told others including her sister, and the connection was established. Had he known, he would surely have had second thoughts about killing a trusting young girl in the pretty straw hat.

A not dissimilar – and equally forgotten – case is that of a seventeen year old Scottish girl Irene Munroe who worked as a typist in London. She was enjoying the first few days of her holiday in Eastbourne in the summer of 1920, when she met two young men who introduced themselves as Jack and Bill.

They were looking for an easy pick-up, and she – apparently flattered by their attentions – unwisely accepted their invitation to go to a public house for a drink. Both men were unemployed (a fact they felt they should conceal); 'Jack', the younger had been in the Navy, and 'Bill', some ten years older and already married, seems to have been very much the senior partner. They saw here a likely prospect. Both were interested in the sexual possibilities, and both were also interested in the girl's handbag which contained what remained of her very · modest holiday money. She found them amusing, and they clearly thought they were in with a chance when she agreed to meet them later for a ramble to Pevensey.

They trudged for some miles along the shingle beach until they found a suitable deserted area. There 'Jack' attacked the girl with a metal-tipped walking stick which he thrust into her mouth, and 'Bill' tried to force her to release her grip on the handbag. But she was tenacious. To stop her screams, 'Bill' picked up a slab of concrete – presumably part of a crumbling breakwater – and killed her with blows to the head. Panicking, they hurriedly did their best to bury the body before other holiday makers came along. It was an altogether poor effort, and they left part of one foot peeping out of the shingle. Then they made off with the handbag and made for their favourite pub where they treated some of the customers. Irene Munroe's tiny savings were not going to last long.

On the following Friday a small boy, playing among the rocks, found firstly a shoe and then a cold stockinged foot protruding,from the shingle. It was not long before the police were at the shallow grave, and were soon inspecting the battered corpse, of Irene Munroe. She was still fully clothed; the only thing that was missing was a handbag. Meanwhile, the dead girl's landlady, a Mrs Wynniatt, could not make out why her lodger hadn't returned to the house. Moreover, a letter had arrived from the dead girl's mother who presumably wanted to know how her daughter was enjoying her holiday. Perhaps she was anxious because in those days it was rather unusual for such young girls to go on holiday alone. And then 'the Wynniatts heard rumours of an unidentified girl's body being found on the beach, so they went to the police.

A Scotland Yard Chief Inspector was soon on the scene, and enquiries were quickly underway both in Eastbourne and in London where Irene Munroe and her mother lived. It did not take the police long to discover that the girl had been seen in the company of two men, and among those questioned were Jack Field and William Gray who – it. later transpired – had both tried to enlist in the Army shortly after the body was discovered. (The Army was not recruiting in large numbers in the aftermath of the First World War – in fact, it was a time of quite large scale demobilization). At first, the two men were allowed to leave but the more the police learned of their spending habits, the more interested they became.

Gradually the pieces of information from various witnesses began to fit. The two men were apprehended,. questioned and charged with murder and theft (whether there had been an attempt at some kind of sexual assault, never became clear). In; December 1920 their trial was conducted at Lewes. The prosecution case was reasonably watertight, and both men were found guilty of murder. The death sentence was mandatory, but the jury added a strong recommendation for mercy on the grounds that the murder was not premeditated. This was ignored and their appeals were dismissed, and both men were duly hanged at Wandsworth Prison in February the following year.

Fascinated as people can be by what we might call the run-of-the-mill case which attracts only passing attention, for good or ill, it is the murder case involving celebrities that usually catches the public imagination. This can happen even where minor aristocracy is concerned as in the case of the Marquis Alain de Bernardy de Sigoyer just after the Second World War. The de Sigoyer case in France coincided with that of the notorious Dr Marcel Petiot who, on the pretence of-helping people escape from German-occupied Paris, killed his victims and disposed of their bodies in his own custom-built mini crematorium after appropriating their money and valuables. The body count is unknown, but the best guess is that he may well have done away with as many as sixty people. Incomprehensibly, the Gestapo had released him in 1943 for lack of evidence, but as the clues mounted, his arrest the following year was inevitable. He was sentenced to death, and Monsieur de Paris (the executioner) had finished his work by five minutes past five on the morning of 26 May 1946. He never did confess or indicate exactly what had happened to all those hopeful travellers and their pathetic belongings. All Petoit would say was, 'When one sets out on a voyage, one takes all one's luggage with one'.

By comparison with Petoit's crimes, de Sigoyer's solitary murder was modest indeed. Yet his rather grotesque career intrigued the public, and his claimed aristocratic status added a certain frisson to the affair. Undoubtedly, his forebears were people of some distinction, and were mainly associated with the legal profession (something of an irony seeing that throughout his lifetime he had been arraigned in so many European courts). But whether the term 'aristocrat' which he proudly used was something of an exaggeration is still somewhat unclear, not least because his early life is something of a mystery.

It is known that he spent much of his childhood in Reuinion, and it may be that it was there that he was influenced by native religious practices which were an uncomfortable amalgam of primitive animism and half-understood Catholicism. It was a syncretistic mix not unlike that of Candomble in modern Brazil, and later came to be seen by critics as a form of 'black magic' – an association that de Sigoyer did not disavow, possibly because it added to his aura of mystery. He left the island in 1919 at the age of fourteen, and spent the next two uneventful years in Bordeaux with an aged aunt. But in 1921, after moving to Toulon, he was in trouble with the police on a charge of confidence trickery (he is said to have pretended to be a public official) and although it was a first offence, was given a short spell in prison. This did nothing to deter him from a versatile life of crime which was punctuated by brief episodes in legitimate employment, often as a salesman. In the following years he travelled widely in France and elsewhere, and was variously charged with disorderly conduct, theft, forgery, demanding money with menaces, and fraud – an impressive career made possible by exemption from military service on conscientious grounds. It was his developing ability to con people which enabled him to live, patently beyond his means, among the minor cosmopolitan set in different parts of post-war Europe.

There is little doubt that his dubious title and winning ways helped him considerably in both his criminal and amatory exploits. It may be too that he occasionally hinted at certain esoteric occult powers and the possibility of rare exotic experiences. Such suggestions – though spurious – were all grist for his duplicitous mill. Certainly, he never seemed to be without a lover: a German actress here, a Romanian official's wife there – anyone who would serve his purposes. In Spain, he founded a 'school of magic' which he claimed was 'purely academic'.

In fact, it smacked strongly of the kind of rigmarole associated with the contemporary Aleistair Crowley's 'Golden Dawn' set-up. But it brought in funds and a sprinkling of female acolytes.

Back in France, he was convicted yet again of fraud, and after much argument at his trial as to whether he was bad or mad, he was committed to an asylum. He later insisted that he had only feigned insanity, nevertheless, he remained in the asylum for six years where he was anything but a pliant patient. He was finally discharged in 1937, and was able to purchase a large house at Hautvillers not far from Paris with money that he had presumably stashed away before his incarceration. The house known as La Maison Rouge was even staffed by a couple of ex-inmates from the asylum. It was a bizarre menage, and eventually excited the attention of the police who were looking for a missing American tourist. They toyed with the idea that de Sigoyer had murdered him and appropriated his property, and even went so far as to dig up part of the garden. It was a fruitless search, and they gave it up after their host disarmingly said 'don't bother to look any more: I ate him'. Instead of taking statements for what it was worth, the police decided to arrest de Sigoyer, and in July 1938 he was again sent to an asylum. He spent only a few months there, and after another minor swindling episode for which he was imprisoned for three months, he was on his way once again.

It was now March 1939, and the political situation was looking decidedly grim. De Sigoyer, however, was soon up to his old games. He had already acquired a mistress, and before long had reverted to the well-tried scam of a 'Centre for Higher Esoteric Studies' while managing a small cafe on the side. One of his new neighbours was a Madame Kergot whose eighteen year'old daughter Janine, caught de Sigoyer's all-too-experienced eye. Within no time at all he had switched mistresses. In October 1939 he and Janine were married – an uncharacteristic deviation from his normal behaviour which suggests that he did have a genuine affection for her *at the time*. As subsequent events would show, it was pretty ephemeral, and hardly compared with her feelings for him. At least, not if her letters are anything to go by.

When the German troops occupied Paris in the middle of June 1940, de Sigoyer continued to manage the cafe While most citizens were content to keep their heads down, he slowly graduated from serving Germans the occasional glass of wine to supplying them with casks wholesale – an act which was tantamount to collaboration. Eventually his new sideline necessitated another move, though only to another outlying area of Paris where he could also rent a warehouse. By late 1940, his household consisted of himself, Janine, their infant son, and a seventeen year old girl, Irene Lebeau, who soon doubled as a servant and in-house mistress.

It hardly needs to be stated that relationships in this ménage à trois were not exactly harmonious. Certainly Janine did not take kindly to her husband's nocturnal excursions to Mlle. Lebeau's boudoir. Indeed, they occasioned what can only be described as a series of brawls, yet this uneasy situation continued for four years. In 1942, Janine had another child, a daughter, and in 1943 Irene Lebeau did likewise. It was then that Janine decided that enough was enough, and obtained a judicial separation. She left to live with her mother, and then fatally as it turned out – was able to get a court order for the payment of,10,000 francs a month. From then onwards whatever affection de Sigoyer had for his wife quickly dissolved. It was not that he was unable to afford the money; in fact, it is estimated that he may have made as much as thirty million francs during the occupation. What he certainly resented was that his wife should take exception to the fact that he had a mistress. After all, wasn't it every Frenchman's right? But what was almost certainly of more concern was that his estranged wife knew too much.

During the hey-day of the occupation his fortunes had obviously flourished. As a collaborator, he would have been persona grata with the authorities, and probably – just in case of any perceived infringements – he had a tacit understanding with the Vichy-influenced police. But as events began to favour the Allies, and a Second Front (the Allied invasion of mainland Europe) could be anticipated at any time, those who had hoped for – or simply expected – a German victory were having to re-think their options. De Sigoyer, rather like Petiot, decided to re-invent himself as a resistant. Yet despite his long experience as a con artist, this was not going to be that simple, especially as his wife and his mistress were both party to his profit-making activities. In these circumstances, the 10,000 francs a month began to look like a form of legal blackmail. It was then that he callously determined that Janine would have to go.

Her murder was directly precipitated by a reminder to her husband that he was behind in his payments. It was well within his means (by this time he was the owner of several properties), but if he delayed or objected and Janine revealed everything she knew, especially to the increasingly powerful resistance movement, he was in serious trouble. Indeed, liquidation might possibly be on the cards; it was not unknown for collaborators to be eliminated. There would be no trial or prolonged examination. The resistance got rid of people without the fuss of visible compunction.

De Sigoyer found a pretext for inviting his wife to his warehouse on the 28th March 1944 where he had already dug a pit to take her body. Irene Lebeau discreetly absented herself to another room, yet quite inexplicably her lover invited her to witness the crime. So much of what we know about the murder derives from her testimony. She certainly witnessed the strangulation, but to what extent she can be regarded as a *willing* accomplice will never be known. At de Sigoyer's trial he gave a somewhat different version, yet it was Irene Lebeau's account that the court accepted and she was acquitted of all complicity in the crime.

De Sigoyer's interrogation by the police was purportedly a very brutal affair. His little card identifying him as a German agent did him no good, but by all accounts he stood up well to the kicks and blows of the police functionaries who had taken their cues from the Gestapo at the notorious avenue Henri-Martin. Yet he still disclaimed any knowledge of his missing wife. To add to his agony, he discovered while in prison that Mlle. Lebeau, like a good patriot, had managed to get herself engaged to a member of the resistance – an association he tried vainly to end. His frantic letters written from a prison cell had little effect on his ex-lover. His time was yesterday. Appeals to the past were lost on those who were beginning to sense the possibility of a new future now that the Allies had landed in France.

When Janine's decomposing body was finally found in April 1945, de Sigoyer still denied any knowledge of how she had died, insisting that theirs was a 'mystical union' which he would never violate. Needless to say, the practised fraudster's pseudo explanations got him nowhere. Any mention of the occult and paranormal powers was now going to do him more harm than good.

There were unreasonable delays (France now had more on its mind than the indiscretions – no matter how serious – of one minor aristocrat), but eventually de,Sigoyer's trial was set for December 19th 1946. He was dignified and urbane in court, as befits a Marquis, real or otherwise. Certainly his behaviour was nothing like that of the angry, demonstrative Petiot – not even when confronted by his former lover's simple but convincing account of the murder. His defence was that she, not he, was the person who was really responsible for the crime. She had shot Janine – he insisted – at the culmination of a furious argument between them.

It was a hopeless defence. There was no forensic evidence to support the idea of a shooting. Pathology was just not on his side. The court acquitted,the girl, found de Sigoyer guilty of murder and he was sentenced to death – one of scores of collaborators at this time. Sentence was carried out at 4.59 a.m. at Sante Prison on June 11th 1947. He died courageously and unceremoniously like many an aristocrat in the Revolution with whom, in his last moments he may have felt some affinity.

The de Sigoyer case may be compared and contrasted with two further more recent cases which again illustrate – though in quite different ways – how murder is committed out of fear of exposure. The first sometimes misleadingly called 'The CBS Murders Case' by the media, understandably so as media personnel were tragically involved, although they were not the main focus of the crime. In terms of motive it does have something in common with the de Sigoyer case.

Irwin Margolies was an apparently prosperous jewellery manufacturer in New York city, but it transpired that much of his wealth had been obtained by fraud. His accountant, Margaret Barbera, knew about it, and Margolies became convinced that before long she might either be tempted to blackmail him, or reveal all – or both. He thought at first of arranging things so that if all was revealed she could be blamed for the fraud. He agonized about it, and then decided to go for broke and have her killed. Consequently he hired a petty criminal, Donald Nash, to. do the job for a modest $8000.

Nash took his time and first of all murdered a friend and confidante of Margaret Barbera called Jenny Soo Chin on the assumption that she too was aware of Margolies' misdemeanours. He then waited some time before ensnaring and shooting the thirty-seven year old accountant as she was about to get into her car in a car park at Pier 92 on April 12th 1982. But some CBS employees who had come for their cars happened to see Nash moving the body. They were unable to avoid detection by the killer who shot and killed three of them, presumably with a silenced automatic, but a fourth was able to escape and saw the gunman making his getaway in a van.

This was Nash's undoing. His van was traced, and he was arrested by the police. In May 1983 he was found guilty on four – though it should have been *five* – charges of murder and given a 108 year sentence. Margolies, already in prison for fraud, was also found guilty and given 50 years.

Another case which was something of a cause celèbre in France is also all about fear of exposure but here the circumstances were quite different. For some eighteen years Jean-Claude Romand lived a lie. Not even his closest relatives and friends knew – or apparently even guessed – that the man they thought worked as a doctor for the World Health Organization was in fact, a fake. It was believed that he was engaged in important drug research, that he attended various international conferences, and was a respected medical figure who moved among the humanitarian community.

None of this was true. He was not a doctor, was not involved in drugs research, and did not belong to any international organization. In fact, when he left his house in the morning, he simply whiled away his time going for walks and reading magazines. He financed this rather aimless lifestyle by embezzling money which family and friends had handed over to him for investment in entirely fictitious companies The amazing thing is that he was able to dupe so many people for so long. It was when people began pressing him for some return on their investments, that life inevitably became difficult.

It reached an intolerable level when his mistress actually asked for her money back. But he couldn't face the prospect of revealing all to those who loved and trusted him to safeguard their pensions and savings. It was easier to lie than confess. Rather than endure the shame, he decided to kill his family and then commit suicide (but why not *just* commit suicide?). He battered his wife to death, shot his children after watching TV with them, and then drove to Paris and shot his parents and attacked his mistress. On returning home he swallowed barbiturates and set fire to the house. Perhaps unfortunately, he was rescued in a coma, and was later able to divulge everything that had happened. It had all started, he said, with *one* lie which escalated into wholesale deception and murder.

viii) MURDER BY CONTRACT

We hear a great deal these days about serial killers – a type that has become a staple of the popular media. It is opportunistically felt that serial killing is such a bizarre phenomenon that it pays to cash in on the public's fascination with that which is both horrible and intriguing. But in many ways murder by contract, which is less well known, suggests a cold and impersonal anonymity that is even more chilling than the run-of-the-mill serial killing. For here we encounter the person who is given a commission and who rarely asks questions. The direction from above – the person who orders the 'hit' – is enough. A price is agreed, and a timetable may be set. Even the method may not be pre-determined. It is not a question of whether or not the 'mark' deserves to be killed, or whether he or she could claim mitigating circumstances. None of these things makes any difference. So Albert Anastasia (commonly known as the 'Mad Hatter' of whom we shall hear more) could order the execution of innocent, civic minded, Arnold Schuster in 1952 simply because Schuster had identified a much -wanted bank robber, Willie Sutton, who was subsequently arrested. Neither Schuster nor Sutton meant anything to Anastasia, but the 'hit' was ordered because the crime boss protested that he didn't like 'squealers'. It did Anastasia no good, as it merely added to his growing reputation for instability – a tendency that was not welcome among his fellow racketeers. Killings in the course of 'business' were one thing, but unnecessary murders inevitably invited unwanted attention.

In 1940, a well-known criminal, Abraham Reles (known commonly as 'Kid Twist'), was arrested on a number of serious charges including possession of narcotics, and decided to do a deal with his prosecutors.

He had already served several terms in prison, and knew that' if he was convicted this time he was in for a very long stretch – perhaps even for life. So in exchange for certain exemptions he said he could give the police information about a series of crimes by an organization of which they were barely aware – one that came to be dubbed Murder Incorporated.

The revelations were sensational and concerned an extensive murder by a contract organization which had been set up by big-time crime bosses some years before in order to protect their various illicit interests. Early on in the Thirties it had been decided to end the feuding between various criminal factions which had been a feature of the Prohibition era. During the palmy days of Prohibition, it is estimated that deaths from alcoholism in Chicago alone rose by 600 per cent by 1927, and that by 1930 some thirty-five thousand Americans had been killed by poison liquor supplied largely from the illicit stills of the bootleggers, and thousands more were left blinded and crippled by damaged nervous systems (Allsop, 1962, p.36). So why did it continue? Quite simply – as statistics clearly show – because the people wanted it. They were well aware to the dangers. As a popular song of the period expressed it in 1928:

Keep away from bootleg hooch
When you're on the spree
Take good care of yourself
You belong to me

As Al Capone the crime Tsar of Chicago put it when accused of running a criminal empire which also included gambling and prostitution, 'I simply give the people what they want'.

During the fourteen years of Prohibition competition was fierce among the various criminal gangs. Again, in Chicago alone, there were 703 gangland murders for which no one was successfully convicted. It was the scene of the typical one-way ride – the occupational hazard of those involved in the precarious but lucrative profession of giving the people what they wanted. As Benjamin ('Bugsy') Siegal, one of the most notorious gangsters to survive the era, said to a nervous acquaintance, 'Don't worry, we only kill one another'.

At the demise of Prohibition, some of the most ruthless – yet rational-racketeers decided on two things: first they had to diversify – they had to find new ways, both legitimate and illegitimate ways of making money. Second, the rivalry had to cease; there were easy pickings for everyone if those concerned were prepared to organize on a sensible basis. Thus a near-enough national criminal organization was born which, under the leadership of its 'council' was to control vice – pre-eminently gambling, prostitution and drugs for the indefinite future.

Unsurprisingly, the transition was not without its growing pains – not to say, fatalities. As was to be expected, not everyone was in agreement with the new arrangements. From 1928 the conflict became increasingly acrimonious. So much so, in fact, that a conference was called in Atlantic City in 1929 in order to iron out at least some of the difficulties. It was well attended by crime bosses from much of the USA. But there were still sharp divisions, mainly between the old-style gangsters headed by such people as Joe Masseria and Salvatore Maranzone (though surprisingly not Al Capone) who were not too keen on the idea of a national cartel, and the up-and-coming 'rationalizers' such as Charles 'Lucky Luciano, Joe Adonis (real name Guiseppe Doto), Albert Anastasia and their acolytes. There was a nominal agreement on the formation of a syndicate, but the eventual outcome was a certain amount of blood-letting as these notables jockeyed for power in what became known as the Castellammarese War (1928-31). Both Masseria and Maranzano were killed, together with a number of their minions, and the Syndicate (aka Organization) was born.

The Syndicate was formed mainly by Sicilians and Italians (its Mafia core), but it also included important Jewish elements together with some marginal Jewish mobsters. Its ostensible purpose was to so organize crime across the USA that new money-making avenues would be explored so that profits might be maximized. But how was the organization to be defended, and how were its members to be disciplined? It was at this point that Anastasia, who had originally been Adonis' enforcer, either personally or in concert with others came up with the idea of a kind of murder agency which would ensure that everyone observed the Council's rules. With the Council's imprimatur (and this had to be sought) torture and murder were the fate-of all those who stepped out of line or in any way betrayed or-jeopardised the Organization.

Murder Inc. had already been anticipated by the Bugs-Meyer gang in the 1920s, led – as the name suggests – by Bugsy Siegel (who may well have been involved in the infamous Saint Valentine's Day Massacre in 1929 which was almost certainly ordered by Capone) and Meyer Lansky who was later to be the key financial organiser in the Syndicate. In its revised form it consisted mainly of Jewish-Italian killers drawn from East New York which included among others Seymour 'Blue Jaw' Magoon, Harry 'Happy' Maione, Mostel Goldstein, Frank 'The Dasher' Abbandando, the ominously called Albert 'Tick Tock' Tannenbaum, Harry Strauss, Mendy Weiss, Frankie Carbo and of course Reles himself. Anastasia was nicknamed the 'Lord High Executioner' and he appears to have shared authority with Louis 'Lepke' Buchalter who was no stranger to the earlier New York gang wars. Like the others, Buchalter – a diminutive figure, had started as a petty criminal and had graduated to the big-time of bootlegging, protection rackets, and labour racketeering especially in connection with the garment industry. In his hey-day he employed a host of minor legmen and subsidiary enforcers who knew it was more than their lives were worth to cross their employer. In one instance, Buchalter's contact man with the unions who was known to be drinking heavily and talking imprudently to the wrong people, was killed on Buchalter's orders. In another, an accomplice who had skimmed some of the profits from a $10 million drugs deal was found stabbed and covered in cement in the East River. For a while Buchalter acted as chairman of the Council of the Syndicate which by 1934 had become an established entity, recognized by criminal elements as far as the West Coast. Its edicts were enforced by the security arm (Murder Inc.) which in less than ten years claimed hundreds of lives; indeed, the final tally will never be known.

In its early days it received its assignments to murder people who were deemed a danger to the organization who lived within the New York area. Often such people were known to the killers because they too were part of the criminal fraternity. Later the scope of their operations widened, and they would be instructed to dispose of individuals almost anywhere in the country. Indeed, it became policy to import killers from one area to 'hit' someone in another area and then disappear again. This obviously made detection that much more difficult. Discovery was also inhibited by either hiding, torching or drowning the bodies of victims. A typical 'hit' was that of Walter Sage who was in charge of the Syndicate's slot machine operations in Upper New York State. In 1937, he was suspected of skimming the profits, so four 'professionals' took Sage for a ride. He was stabbed with an ice pick (one of Murder Inc's favourite weapons). The body was then tied to a pinball machine, rowed to the middle of a lake and dumped. This is one of the main reasons why the police were slow to cotton on to the fact that such a murder organization was at work. Actual dismemberment was not unknown – a task undertaken by a group which 'Orient Express'-like would make the killing something of a gruesome orgy, even inviting lady friends (an. imprudent innovation) to assist in the horrifying ritual. Yet sometimes the killings were open and much more matter-of-fact. Also in 1937, Strauss and Maione were dispatched to Detroit where they shot, one, Harry Millman, in a restaurant in full view of the customers and coolly walked out again.

Murder Inc. had its own terms of employment and rates of remuneration. Besides a regular retainer for pocket money between assignments, each person received between $1000 and $5000 for a killing. Business was so brisk that each man was able to live in some style. If there were hitches such as prosecutions or spells in prison, members were assured of competent legal representation, and there was always insurance and compensation for wives and families – and, if necessary, widows. Indeed, within the Fraternity, contract murder came to be regarded as such a lucrative occupation that the organization was never short of recruits. After all, the money was good, and it held out attractive possibilities for those who were keen to join those 'men of respect' in the upper echelons of the Syndicate. Killing held no qualms for these young aspirants who were only too anxious to prove themselves to their superiors. Young assassins- such as George Young and Joseph Schaefer seemed to be genuinely enthusiastic at the prospect of emulating top killers like Harry Strauss who could calmly axe a man to death in a cinema and nonchalently leave with the screaming crowd.

Harry Strauss (sometimes known as 'Pittsburg Phil' or simply as -'Pep') was as pathological as they come. Born in 1908 in Brooklyn, as a youth he quickly adapted to the crime culture of the Prohibition era. He specialized in murder in various forms and by various methods, and soon established a reputation as being one of the most competent and sadistic killers within the organization.

By 1930 he is estimated to have murdered at least one hundred people, and quite possibly several times that number. And by 1934, the year that the Syndicate might be said to have achieved nationwide recognition, he had been arrested seven times on various charges, but to the disgust of the police had not been convicted on any of them. It is interesting that when the Police Commissioner in Brooklyn told his officers that Strauss was a hired assassin who deserved to be shot on sight, there were remonstrations by liberals that this would contravene his civil rights. Needless to say, when soon afterwards he was arrested for the eighteenth time on a murder charge, he again walked free.

Strauss was the archetypal killer who appears to have had no reservations about his work. Indeed, the evidence suggests that he positively enjoyed it and took pride in 'artistry' and efficiency. Certainly, he did not evince any remorse, and one suspects that he was – or became – totally impervious to true fellow-feeling. When after 'Kid Twist' Reles' revelations, he was finally indicted for murder in 1940, he tried to convince the court that he was insane. But in spite of his bizarre behaviour and unkempt appearance, the court was unimpressed. He was found guilty of First Degree murder, and died in the electric chair in 1941; fellow killers Harry Maione, Frank Abbandando, Mendy Weiss and Louis Capone were similarly executed shortly afterwards.

Only one of the principals of Murder Inc. was successfully prosecuted – Louis Buchalter. He was already being harrassed by the police for his multifarious criminal activities with his equally lethal partner, Jacob Shapiro. Before his involvement with Murder Inc. was known he went into hiding but in 1939 was persuaded by Anastasia to give himself up on narcotics charges in the hope of an early release, but once the facts were known, no parole was possible and he was executed in 1944. Obviously, Anastasia knew a thing or two. Other key members of the Syndicate, for one reason or another all escaped conviction. Luciano, still a Mafia kingpin, was already in prison, but was paroled after rendering 'services' (that have never been satisfactorily explained) to the US military during the war, after which he was deported to Italy. Adonis, after much litigation, was also deported but not until 1956. Such top crime bosses, were too far removed from the murders they either ordered or condoned to be implicated. Frank Costello (genially known as 'Uncle Frank') had also kept a low profile, and like his fellow crime bosses continued with his covert racketeering activities. In 1957, he narrowly escaped assassination himself and decided – wisely as it turned out – to retire from the 'trade'. Vito Genovese, perhaps the most sinister and unscrupulous of the Council (it was probably Genovese that ordered the 'hit' on Costello) also survived as a crime boss and is believed to have been behind the murders of several of his rivals in the 1950s. He was eventually convicted on several charges in 1959 on the evidence of confessed Mafia gunman, Joseph Valachi, and sent to prison where he died in 1969.

Among others who survived – at least temporarily – one of the most interesting is 'Big Al' himself. Anastasia was a wanted man in the early 1940s, but cunningly and unaccountably became 'lost' – of all places – in the US Army. He later boasted of his quite fictitious exploits abroad, although he actually never left American shores. He was later to take up his chosen profession and his position on the Council, but in time characteristically overreached himself. It was decided, possibly at the instigation of Genovese, that Anastasia represented a threat to the organization. So in October 1957, as the crime boss was having his customary haircut and manicure at New York's Park Sheraton Hotel, two men entered, waived the employees aside, and shot Anastasia to death. His esteem was so low that he didn't even merit the traditional gangster's funeral.

And what of the man who in his revelations to prosecutor, Burton Turkus, had initiated the investigations into Murder Inc. in the first place? 'Kid Twist' Reles who, it transpired, had a remarkable memory for details, dates and victims etc. was prepared to tell all in the hope of immunity. Consequently as a key prosecution witness he was housed under police guard on the sixth floor of the Half Moon Hotel in Coney Island. But the word was out, and a contract rumoured to be,little short of $100,000 – an enormous fee for a 'hit' – was put out, it is said, by Frank Costello. Reles' death was absolutely critical for the Mob because his testimony could have meant the end of so many of the key figures in the Organization. But fortunately for them, the salary of a police enforcement officer was not that generous, and some – or even all – of them who were charged with guarding Reles took the bait. Reles fell to his death from the sixth floor apartment window. It was implausibly maintained that he was trying to escape, and this became the official explanation. But few seriously doubted that he was thrown out no doubt protesting as violently as many of his victims.

Murder is a terrible thing in any circumstances, and murder by contract is both chilling and squalid. Yet one of the most salutary lessons we can learn from this is how many are all too willing to take up the profession if the money and the prospects are right. Racketeering can be – and certainly was a profitable if precarious occupation, especially, if one belonged to a feared hit squad which had its own perverted loyalty system. That is until, for one reason or another (as with Reles and some of his minor associates) it paid to break ranks with all its possible consequences. By all accounts, these men enjoyed their work, and new recruits – of which there was no shortage – were only too prepared to ingratiate themselves with the 'dons' who had such awesome reputations. There has to be something frighteningly evil about humans who can no longer feel pity or be moved by a fellow human's suffering.

ix) MURDER AND POLITICAL EXPEDIENCY

The history of what we might designate as political murder goes back into the indefinite past. Conspiracies to overthrow rulers as in a coup d'etat, or simply to eliminate key political figures can certainly be found as far back as the Egyptian New Kingdom (it may well be that the best known of the Pharaohs, Tutankhamun, was himself the victim of just such a plot). Throughout history there have been countless incidents of political murder – often dignified by the slightly less harsh term, assassination. Often these have not been the random acts of unbalanced fanatics, but carefully worked out plots by influential agencies which have been calculated to eliminate what is believed to be some actual or potential danger.

In one form or another this sort of thing has been happening throughout history. Giovanni Fogliani was a leading citizen of the Italian city of Fermo in the 15th Century. He had adopted his orphaned nephew,' Oliverotto, and when the youth was old enough he had sent him to join a then well-known condotierre, Paulo Vitelli, during the seemingly interminable wars between various Italian city-states. Service with such an accomplished mercenary captain was felt to be good training for a young man in these troubled times. In 1501, after some years of fighting, Oliverotto returned home, thoroughly brutalized, with plans set for his own future. He was about to show his gratitude for his uncle's generosity.

He asked his uncle to organize a banquet to celebrate his homecoming. Giovanni prepared a sumptuous feast and invited not only relatives, but also many of Fermo's most eminent citizens. When Oliverotto arrived he was accompanied by a well accoutred entourage of guards and servants, and his wealth was such that he was in a position to pay for the celebrations himself. The citizens were duly impressed, though no doubt one or two wondered how he could have come by so much money in such a short time. Perhaps they were not aware that successful mercenary captains could very soon be rich with booty.

But they didn't have to wonder too long. At some point during the feast Oliverotto gave a pre-arranged signal to his soldiers and they butchered everyone there, including the elderly Giovanni. Oliverotto and his men then rode to the cityhall,_ and demanded that the city's officials recognise him as Prince. They had little choice as most of the members of the elected council were now dead. Some did refuse, and were killed immediately. He then proceeded to set up his own institutions of government. Anyone who resisted was brutally dealt with; all others were forced to comply.

And then came a misjudgement. Instead of being content with what he had so ruthlessly acquired, and settling down to rule the city, after a few months he decided to join his old comrade-in-arms, Vitelli, for more fighting and.pillaging. Perhaps the excitement of that kind of life gets into the blood. But it was a mistake. Very shortly afterwards he was dead (1502) at the hands of an even more treacherous military captain, Cesare Borgia, who spent much of his short life extending the territorial possessions of the Papacy. At least, Fermo was able to resume its traditional ways, untroubled by the depredations of ambitious military dynasts.

At about the same time that great enemy of the West, Turkey, was having its own dynastic problems. The Turks were still culturally a nomadic people with an unenviable reputation for belligerence and expansionism. Their Sultan, Bayazid II, pursued an active foreign policy of opportunistic aggression. But the Sultan, now well past his prime, was about to be usurped by his son, Selim, now a man in his forties, and avaricious for the power which he felt had long been denied him. In 1512, he enlisted the help of some of the younger officers in the army, and Bayazid was faced with a fait accompli. At first, it appeared to be a simple, bloodless coup d'etat. But Selim meant to consolidate his position. At a celebratory feast, Selim had his father poisoned. Then he ordered the execution of all his brothers and nephews (a practice that was to become well known as an Ottoman trademark). No one was going to be allowed to live who might threaten his position, so any officials of state who resisted the takeover were also put to the sword;

Now Sultan, Selim (soon to be known to his contemporaries as Selim the Grim) led his armies to Mesopotamia, Armenia and Egypt, and won a series of notable victories. He defeated the last of the decadent Abbasid dynasty, and assumed the title of Caliph which gave him pre-eminence in the Muslim world – a position he was able to bestow on his son, Suleiman the Magnificent. Before his death in 1521, he had made himself virtually unassailable by a combination of guile and extreme cruelty which probably exceeded that of any of his successors, none of whom was that squeamish.

This kind of tale could be repeated over and over again. Where power is sought, murder – possibly on the grand scale – can be rationalized in the interests of political expediency. Few states exemplify the persistence of this phenomenon more than certain countries in Latin America where the ursurpation of power was something of a national sport. For example, in 1816 Jose Francia led a movement in Paraguay to overthrow Spanish colonial rule. Francia, an able and learned man, was also one of the most devious men in South American politics. He helped rebels to establish a republic, but at the same time played one group off against another by making irreconcilable concessionary promises to each faction. Ostensibly following ancient Roman practice, Francia should have acted as 'Consul' for one year only, but in that year he reorganized the state in such a way that he could not easily be ousted from power. He dismissed all potential rivals within the military, and set up his own security police force. He then handpicked his own Congress and had himself 'elected' Dictator for Life. In his way he emulated Roman military dynasts such as Pompey and Caesar who under the constitution were supposed only to hold dictatorial power (imperium) for six months. His dictatorship resulted in the ruthless suppression of all resistance. The fear of his anger among his subordinates indirectly led to his death. He fell down in a fit while conducting an interview, but a guard was afraid to fetch help because he had received no direct orders to do so. In such bizarre circumstances the Dictator died – a situation slightly reminiscent of the circumstances attending the death of Stalin.

To give a near contemporary example, in 1873, power was usurped in Guatemala by Justo Rufino Barrios. He had previously led a coup d'etat which had ousted one President and installed another, President Granodos. The loyal Barrios was then made Commander-in-Chief of the Army, and within two years he had removed Granodos and assumed power himself. Like, Francia, he then redrew the Constitution and proclaimed himself Dictator. But unlike Francia, he overreached himself and lost his life trying to extend his rule to other neighbouring states in 1885.

At almost the same time, a similar set of circumstances obtained in Venezuela, one of the first Spanish American colonies to rebel against their overlords. Venezuela declared independence in 1811, but the rebels did not succeed in driving out Spanish troops until 1821. Nevertheless, the country remained desperately unstable for some years, and even during the government of President Monagas (1849-59), the country was in a state of near anarchy. Minor rebellions and banditry under would-be war lords were common. It was during this period that Antonio Blanko – somewhat more ruthless than the rest – successfully bribed and fought his way to power. By a series of astute moves whereby he accumulated considerable wealth, he was finally able to engineer a coup in 1870 which resulted in the abolition of the entire government. As effective Dictator, he commanded a state which became a byword for greed and corruption. His nepotistic regime encouraged any venture which brought in more wealth; whether it was legitimate or otherwise was of little concern. What mattered were results. In his case, crime certainly paid. By 1889, corruption had reached such an intolerable level that he was forced from power. by a rebellion of the Creoles" Venezuelans of European descent, yet he was still able to retire to Britain with most of his ill-gotten gains. Needless to say, as was so common in Latin America, control then passed into the all-too-willing hands of the military.

Few states exemplify the political expediency theme better than Mexico. In 1855, the government of Mexico proposed radical changes to the very wealthy Catholic Church. This led to political instability and finally to civil war. The reforming party was led by the people's champion, Benito Juarez, who was joined by his successful military leader, Profirio Diaz. As a counter-measure in 1860, French troops, with little concern for international legality, invaded Mexico ostensibly in order to protect French interests which it was feared would be jeopardized if the country remained in the hands of a revolutionary government. So they and the powerful clerical party installed the Austrian Archduke Maximillian as Emperor, a hapless foreigner who naturally did not commend himself to the Mexican people.

But the struggle continued, and in 1867, the Archduke was captured and unnecessarily executed by the Juarist government which then implemented the proposed reforms. However, when Juarez offered himself for re-election as President in 1871, he found himself opposed by his erstwhile colleague, Diaz, and although his campaign against Diaz was successful, the episode understandably forced a breach between the one-time confederates, and friendship turned to bitterness. When Juarez died the following year, he was replaced not by Diaz but by a candidate who had nothing like the support of his predecessor. What is more he was detested by Diaz; the scene was set for a further civil war; Former soldiers rallied to the rebel cause led by Diaz, and together they defeated the government forces after a protracted struggle in 1876.

Diaz became President, theoretically an elected office, but step by step Diaz transformed it into a self-perpetuating dictatorship. It was a not untypical example of how as a form of role reversal the gamekeeper becomes the poacher. He mobilized some of the more disreputable elements in the country (bandits, criminals, etc.) of which there was no apparent shortage, and these became the core of a security police organization which he used to suppress all opposition.

Diaz, who liked to display himself in over-medalled regalia, at least gave the country some measure of stability, and with it a modest degree of prosperity – even if the wealth did find its way into' very few hands. But with time came disaffection within his own ranks, and in 1910 he was forced to resign and fled not exactly penniless to France, and was succeeded by Francisco Madero who ushered in a new period of anarchy and bloodshed. The Mexican people were to discover yet again that no matter who is in power, the lot of the ordinary peasant never changes.

Madero (b.1873) became involved in local politics as a youth, and when still a young man assumed the leadership of the Independent Party which was opposed to the policies and practices of the Diaz regime. At the age of only thirty-seven, he became a candidate for the Presidency in 1910, campaigning on a platform of greater rights for the people – always a good ploy in the election stakes. But before the elections were held, he was arrested by Diaz's security police and detained until the voting was over. Needless to say, Diaz remained in power. As soon as he was released from detention, Madero was intent on fomenting political unrest which eventually led to open rebellion. Diaz was caught uncharacteristically on the wrong foot. In his complacency he had not bargained for such a powerful opposition; he felt that the benefits he had brought to Mexico would outweigh the effect of the oppressive means whereby they had been achieved. He was forced to flee the country, as we have seen, and Madero took over the Presidency.

Madero embarked on a series of reforms which were ostensibly intended to bring greater liberty and prosperity to the people. But the attempted transition which necessarily involved some relaxation of control, simply meant that the state degenerated into anarchy and yet further civil war. As with the endeavours of so many reformers where the cancellation of debt is the intractable problem, Madero's efforts finally pleased no one. The wealthier classes were patently unsympathetic, and the people, impatient for change, continued to be discontented because the reforms were not as radical as they had hoped. The disillusioned Madero was murdered by his opponents in February 1913.

Madero's successor made no pretence of being a champion, of the people. And he was certainly no aspiring politician from the conventional mould. Francisco Pancho Villa was – and continued to be – an unrepentant bandit. His speciality was banks and other similar targets. He was astute and ruthless, and he and his formidable gang of bandittos were too much for any local force. Indeed, try as he did, Diaz even with government troops at his disposal was never able to apprehend Villa. And when Madero took over, he made the classic error of pardoning Villa and his men which gave them the opportunity of reforming and enlarging their forces and continuing on their merry way. Villa was now effectively a kind of minor warlord with a small army at his command. Mexico was now in such a turmoil that Villa could afford to ignore the dictates of the central government, and he was powerful enough in 1911 to set himself up as 'governor' of an independent state in the north of the country. Once Madero was dead, Villa used his considerable muscle to influence the choice of the new President, Venustiano Carranza, but contrary to his expectations, Carranza was unwilling to reward Villa's services. This was a recipe for yet more carnage.

In October 1914, Villa raised another rebellion, and his bandit army was able to crush the government forces that were doing their best to restore some semblance of order. He set up a puppet government under his personal appointee, But Carranza was still free, and was still recognized in the USA as the legitimate President. In 1916, Carranza set to work to neutralize all Villa's gains. He was able to mobilize support from those who by now were heartily sick of bandit rule; Villa's cruelties had alienated many of those who had once sympathized with his anti-government stance.

Carranza embarked on a long and successful campaign to recapture all that he had lost. Villa was at last proscribed as an outlaw and retreated to his northern territory from which he was still able to wage a, savage guerrilla war against the forces of authority. He still managed to elude capture, and in 1920 when Carranza was murdered, the new government offered Villa a massive bribe to cease operations. Surprisingly, the bandit, now in his forties, agreed, took the money, and retired to a ranch. Yet one suspects that this was simply a government awaiting its opportunity. With most of Villa's forces disbanded, he was all too vulnerable, and within three years he was dead (1923). The government had paid its debt.

Villa's career was indissolubly linked with that of his slightly younger and – if anything – more ruthless contemporary, Emiliano Zapata, who has been called 'possibly the most powerful bandit ever to use a gun' (Matthews, 1989 p. 307). Zapata,(b.1879) was from Indian peasant stock and like his people lived in abject poverty in his early years. Mexican peasants, rather like their medieval European counterparts, were tied to the land and were, by and large, unfeelingly exploited by the landlords. It was obviously in the interests of the wealthier classes to maintain the peasants (peons) in a state of subjection in order to maximize their profits and to enhance their own status vis-a-vis the proletariat (if indeed the peasants could rightly be categorized as proletarian seeing as their menial status was more like that of serfs). Even Diaz who – as we have seen – began his career as something of a revolutionary ensured that the Indian peasant population was kept in its place.

Once Diaz had been overthrown in 1911, Zapata raised a rebellion among the Indians (strictly, the indigenes), and with a force of several hundreds went on the rampage ostensibly in the cause of 'freedom'. But the struggle for liberty can be merely an excuse for plunder and murder. Certainly Zapata and his men took bloody revenge on those they saw as their persecutors. Ranches were raided, homes burned, and property pillaged in order to finance further depredations. Zapata's aims and methods were so obviously akin to those of Pancho Villa that after President Modero was murdered in 1913, the two joined forces and put Carranza in power.

The new President, however, failed to live up to expectations. The peasants remained discontented because Carranza failed to implement the promised reforms. So again Zapata and his Indian supporters rebelled. With his brother, Eufermio, he commanded an army of some 20,000 men which maurauded the length and breadth of the country spreading death and destruction wherever they went. At one point it is said that Zapata controlled seventy per cent of

Mexico, and was able to appoint two Presidents, and powerful enough to dismiss them when they displeased him.

A considerable body of romantic myths in both books and films have surrounded Zapata, as they have about other so-called heroic figures of a similar kind (compare Salvatore Guiliano in Sicily)..But he was no more than a charismatic brigand. He led a life of astounding extravagance and licentiousness. Much of the money he extorted is known to have been squandered on women and drink. In short, his lifestyle was quite unlike that of his fellow peasants in whose interests he was supposed to be fighting. More damning is his record of theft and destruction. He is estimated to have caused a quarter of a million dollars worth of damage, and ordered the execution of some 11,000 people, many of whom he is said to have killed personally.

He eventually fell out with Villa when their interests diverged. Rivalry between such similar personalities was almost bound to develop sooner or later. This inevitably began to limit his power, and once Villa and Carranza had come to terms, Zapata's fate was effectively sealed. He was led into a trap by government forces (federales) in 1918 and shot to death. The view was – perhaps rightly – that any kind of trial would have been pointless, and that summary justice was no more than he deserved.

Throughout history there have been countless murders in the interests of political expediency. In modern times too, these have been perpetrated where some form of usurpation or coup d'etat has been intended or successfully carried out. Sometimes it has been the case of getting rid of some potential rival or a known or believed traitor within the system. In totalitarian regimes such as those in Nazi Germany and Soviet Russia, loyalty to the state could be very widely interpreted indeed. So we have Hitler's elimination of the SA leadership in the 'Night of the Long Knives' in June 1934; and we have Stalin's ruthless purges of the Party, the military and even the NKVD (secret police) in the late Thirties. More recently we have witnessed the assassination of dissidents abroad by hit-squads from their home countries whether in the old Eastern bloc (e.g. the poison pellet murder in London of Georgi Markov) or in some of the more notorious Middle Eastern states.

Democratic regimes too have not been entirely innocent. The American CIA so it is rumoured – was behind the assassination of President Allende. of Chile Patrice Lumumba of Katanga, and was certainly involved in several attempts to kill Fidel Castro of Cuba.

The CIA may also have been connected – albeit indirectly – with the following outrage concerning the Republic of China.

The case in point is that of the delegates to the Afro-Asian Bandung Conference in 1955. On April 11th, there was a mid-air explosion on the Kashmir Princess, an Air India Constellation over the ocean near Sarawak. It had been chartered by the People's Republic of China to carry delegates from China and Vietnam to the Conference together with a number of correspondents. In all, fifteen people died, but the co-pilot, the navigator and a senior inspector survived. It was a sensational case in which seven countries became involved.

A committee of enquiry was appointed by the Indonesian government to consider the conclusions of the investigating team which fortunately had been able to salvage ninety per cent of the aircraft; Survivors spoke of an explosion in the starboard wing, and of the fire which resulted from the rupture of the fuel tank. They testified too of the skill of the crew who eventually managed to ditch the burning 'plane. The investigators discovered the remains of a timing mechanism which confirmed their initial impression that this was a deliberate act of sabotage.

The Chinese Ministry of Foreign Affairs issued a statement to the effect that this was the work of ousted Chinese Nationalist leader Chiang Kai-Shek, and it transpired that intelligence already existed that some such plot was in the offing. As Hong Kong was involved, the Chinese demanded that the British look into the matter, especially as they believed the main target was their Premier Chou En-lai. The British complied, and all those connected with the servicing of the machine at Hong Kong were investigated. One man was suspected, but when the police went to arrest him it was discovered, that he had stowed away on an aircraft bound for Formosa that same morning.

The British concluded that this man, an agent of Kuomintang (Chinese Nationalist;) Intelligence, had sabotaged the delegates' plane for a payment of 600,000 Hong Kong dollars, and had actually boasted of the deed to others. The Chinese intimated that actually the American CIA had initiated the plot, and the matter was raised in The House of Commons, but nothing was ever proven. The USA was even asked by Great Britain to persuade Chiang Kai-Shek to have the saboteur extradited, but no response was forthcoming. Cooperation could hardly have been expected. There never was any love lost between China and the Nationalists from whom they had wrested power.

Political rivalry in one form-or another is endemic to governmental systems. No type of state is excluded. Despotic sysbems and totalitarian regimes may be significantly worse than others, but democratic systems have not been immune. It was not uncommon in simple pre-industrial societies (NB 19th century Zulu society), and it has been almost de rigueur in a number of complex pre-industrial societies at various times (dynastic Israel, Ptolemaic Egypt, Imperial Rome, etc.). And despite the moral scruples often voiced in current society, it is still sometimes regarded as a simple and 'clean' way of solving an awkward political problem.

EXCURSUS: MURDER BY DEFAULT

Governments and multi-national commercial organizations have often aided and abetted murder on a grand scale, either out of 'economic necessity' or inadvertently by default. They are rarely prepared to admit complicity, and not infrequently are quite adept at covering their tracks by unconvincing excuses and even rank hypocrisy.

Since 1965 when Indonesia under the leadership of General Suharto seized power in East Timor, it is estimated that at least half a million have been murdered by, or with the compliance of, the military. In Java in the mid-1980s, 5,000 people are known to have been killed by government death squads, and mutilated corpses were left in the streets to rot. This operation, Suharto euphemistically – and cynically – described as 'shock therapy'. But it didn't stop there. Since 1990, 2,000 civilians – according to Amnesty International – have been killed in Sumatra. And when a grave containing 200 bodies was unearthed at Aceh, Indonesian General Pramono was tackled about this, he disputed the figure saying that it was difficult to establish the exact number 'as all the arms and legs were mixed up'.

Few nations have been as casual about mass murder as Indonesia. In Dili, East Timor, troops were not deterred from massacring some 250 people even with a foreign film crew present (note John Pilger's film (Death by a Nation'). Every kind of human rights abuse has been identified from imprisonment without trial, rape and unjustified torture to murder, all with the connivance of the courts. And this is to say nothing of those who have died of starvation. The government has used any means it chose to suppress dissent even of the most minor sort. It has not been just a matter of maintaining unquestioned power, but also of preserving the requisite ideology. Needless to say, this generated a pervasive climate of fear. But when news of these gross abuses reached the outside world, little was done at an official level. International agencies such as Amnesty brought clear evidence of these atrocities to various governments, and although numbers of individuals responded by sending letters of protest, there was still no official action.

Western governments have often been found giving what they regard as salutary advice to the Third World, and – to be fair – many (especially Britain and the USA) have been generous in funding projects in Third World countries. But at the same time as they do so, they can be found driving these impoverished nations into further debt, particularly by selling them arms. This was the case with Indonesia. In 1991, the British Prime Minister, John Major, finalized a deal with Indonesia's Trade and Industry minister for the sale of forty Hawk jets. In mitigation, Whitehall made the preposterous statement that these military aircraft would not be used against civilians. Was this a policy they could guarantee? Indeed, the Indonesian Ministry made it clear that the jets would be used both to train pilots and for ground attack operations. And where would this be if not in East Timor?

Even the UN Commission for Human Rights (of which Indonesia is a member) adopted a 'wait and see' policy. Admittedly, Australia sent troops on a peace-keeping exercise, but by that time the worst had happened. Its all very reminiscent of times past when governments have been apprised of the most fearful atrocities in other parts of the world, and have either not acted at all or have acted too late. The view being that these are domestic affairs into which outsiders must not interfere (Saddam Hussein's persecution of the Kurds), or that it is too difficult (the Allies failure to bomb the Nazi extermination camps), or that its an intractable faraway situation (the massacres in Rwanda and Burundi), or that it might create an 'international situation' by drawing in other powers (the genocide by the Khmer Rouge in Cambodia).

Admittedly, these issues have their own politico-economic rationalities. Governments both East and West, are concerned to protect their own interests. This has to be their primary raison d'etre. Not only do they often neglect what many would consider their belated post-colonial obligations to the Third World, but – as we have seen – they can also be cynically exploitative, especially with respect to the arms trade. This is not to suggest that the armaments industry is wholly anathema, but the sale of arms to demonstrably aggressor nations simply to keep domestic economies viable, begs just too many questions.

Yet we must admit that the problem is not entirely one-sided. Its all really a re-run of the 'whiskey and guns' controversy in relation to the indigenes whom we now erroneously refer to as 'Native Americans'. This trade – if it can be thus dignified – was a two-sided affair. It was a question of supply and demand. It is all very well for anti-capitalists and the like to bleat about the evils of globalization which undoubtedly exist, but as a general rule once Third World States are introduced to the advantages of Western technology they are reluctant to revert to the old ways. Only grossly ill-informed people prefer witchcraft to antibiotics, even if the exchange does mean taking Coca-Cola or Kalashnikovs as part of the package.

MURDER AND IDEOLOGY

On the evenings of the 4th and 5th of December 2000 the BBC screened two programmes entitled 'Horror in the East'. These showed in graphic detail some of the atrocities perpetrated against Allied prisoners by the Japanese during the Second World War (though it was also keen to show that the atrocities were not always on one side). Ostensibly, the main point of the programmes was one of motivation. How was it that' human beings could be so bestial to one another? And the answer – if it is an answer – was that it resulted from an ideology which regarded the enemy as sub-human (i-.e. Japanese vis-a-vis Chinese, and later the Americans vis-a-vis the Japanese) or as otherwise deserving of contempt (Japanese vis-a-vis Allied soldiers who had surrendered). The Japanese, in particular, were seen as having undergone a notably ruthless form of military indoctrination which regarded duty to the Emperor as the cardinal and overriding principle. This military ethic was the only code, and this rendered all other moral scruples null and void. Rape, torture, and murder were inconsequential as far as the enemy were concerned if they served the interests of the Imperial State. And this was not specifically an anti-white or anti-Western policy despite their claim to found a Far Eastern Co-Prosperity Sphere. Note what they did to other Asiatics, especially in the Philippines

But does this really explain the cruelties? Why did such an ethic have such a ready resonance? Can we go along with Professor Robert Hare's contention that maybe as many as one in a hundred people (some experts argue for one in *two* hundred) are psychopaths? And can this really be discerned from brain scans? If so, are we to suppose that fortuitously all those Japanese troops who were responsible for untold atrocities just happened to be those very people? Similarly, did the German SS/SD formations just happen to recruit only the one per cent that were suitable to carry out Hitler's policy of mass murder? The statistical improbabilities are obvious.

We find the same behavioural trends from earliest times, both in relation to war and – more arguably – in relation to human sacrifice which itself was a function of particular forms of ideology. To take just one example from the little known pre Inca Andean civilizations which have left us relatively few artefacts in the Casma Valley. In this site from what is known as the Initial Period, we find artefacts which are devoted to war and the treatment of prisoners. It is believed that these are mainly historical (as opposed to mythological) scenes, and victorious warriors are shown with decapitated heads hanging from their belts. The defeated are portrayed as naked in positions which graphically express their agonies. Nude bodies are shown with eyes bulging and hands flailing, and their torsos sliced in two by transverse cuts. We are speaking here of what are obviously 'trophy-head' cultures, so the bodies are often depicted without heads, sometimes with blood and entrails gushing from the victims. Other sculptures depict severed body parts such as arms, legs, and rows of eyes scattered on the ground (Burger, 1995, pp.78-9).

It is quite clear from these gruesome images that these cultures took a positive delight in their work, not unlike some of the more notorious serial killers of our own time. One is left wondering not only how people can do such things, but also how they can ever come to believe it to be right and even pleasurable to do them. And this is by no means a one off case. Scenes like this have been repeated throughout history, from the mounds of heads left by the Mongols and Tartars to the mass slaughter perpetrated by the Khmer Rouge in Cambodia and the Hutu tribes in Rwanda. Death was not only the understandable outcome of warring factions, it was so often accompanied by unnecessary and gratuitous cruelty toward prisoners and defenceless civilians (see Carlton 1994).

Here; then, we are particularly interested in death and atrocity and its association with ideology, a belief-system which either necessitates or justifies such acts of criminal behaviour. Indeed, as the judges at the Nuremburg Trials decreed, the waging of aggressive, unprovoked war was itself a criminal act. Perhaps there is no more lethal combination than ideology wedded to policy. In the Russian-German conflict of 1941-45, it was made abundantly clear not just to the SS/SD whose Einsatzgruppen (extermination squads) operated behind the lines, but also to the High Command (OKH) itself that this was to be no ordinary war. The military were instructed to pursue the war with 'unusual hardness'. Any hint of opposition by the enemy population was to be dealt with ruthlessly, 'For the life of a German soldier, a death sentence of from fifty to a hundred Communists (Russians) must be generally deemed commensurate'. It was further ordered that firing squads should aim low so as to inflict stomach wounds; in this way the victims could be buried alive in agony so as to increase 'the deterrent effect'. If children were among the hostages they might therefore be missed, in which case they were to be 'despatched by hand' by the officer in charge of the burial party.

There is evidence that some units took a sadistic pleasure in their work, and some evenings organized 'man hunts' on the slightest pretext, burning down villages and killing the fleeing inhabitants: or they might loot Russian homes for souvenirs which were sent home to relatives and friends in Germany, 'here is a lock of hair from a guerrilla girl. They fight like wild cats, and are quite sub-human:....'.

Mass murder, deportations, deliberate starvation, the burning of schools, were all part of an everyday scene. One young officer who had only recently arrived in the, East was ordered to shoot 350 civilians, including women and children, who were allegedly partisans. At first, he hesitated, but on being told that the penalty for disobedience was death, he finally carried out the order by machine-gun fire. When later he was wounded, he was determined never to go back to the Eastern front again (Clark, 1965; pp.153-4: 193).

This policy – and practice – was justified in a number of ways:

i)   because in circumstances like these, the end justifies the means
ii) because the victims were Communists and were therefore a threat to the New Order in Europe
iii) because the victims were Jews and Slavs they were also sub-human (untermensch), and therefore an undesirable species
iv) because extermination was a 'rational' form of pacification
v)   because in the last resort orders were orders; the policy had been made at the very highest level, and it didn't pay to disobey.

Furthermore, the Germans resorted to what was little more than a legal fiction as far as prisoners of war were concerned. They contended that as the Soviet Union was not a signatory to the Geneva Convention, German forces had no obligation to abide by its principles.

As early as July 1941 – a mere month after hostilities began – OKH issued instructions to the German Army (Wehrmacht) that in keeping with the 'prestige and dignity' of the Army, German soldiers must maintain a distance from their prisoners, and if any of their captives tried to escape they were to be shot without warning. Indeed, it was made clear that any resistance even passive, must be summarily dealt with by use of arms. Actually, prisoners were deprived of all warm clothing, and literally hundreds of thousands froze to death in the Russian winter. For those that survived the cold there was also the paucity of rations; Reichsmarshal Goering cynically remarked that if they had nothing else, they might hopefully end up eating one another.

The dead were burned up by flame throwers, so exact figures for the number of prisoners who died is difficult to assess, but a rough estimate is somewhere in excess of three million. The irony is that those who made it until the end of the war were repatriated and then found themselves sent on Stalin's orders to Siberian prison camps. Stalin suspected anyone who had surrendered. Indeed, capitulation was tantamount to cooperation. So those the Germans had failed to kill were again to suffer persecution by their own people.

The very worst atrocities undoubtedly took place in the East, i.e. Poland and Russia where the SS/SD perpetrated unspeakable-massacres culminating in the mechanised mass murder of the Jews, and others in what we now term the Holocaust. But other parts of occupied Europe did not escape entirely unscathed. Guerrilla warfare, for instance, generated extensive reprisals. The Germans together with Italians and some of their Balkan allies went to considerable lengths to reduce partisan activity, and expended some of their best units – including in Yugoslavia a mountain division and a Waffen (military or armed) SS division – but with only limited success. In 1943, the German commander in the Balkans, General Lohr, ordered a massive campaign against the partisans which also included a purge of all those suspected of aiding the resistance. Hostages were tortured, hanged or shot, and,their property destroyed. And although this posed a moral dilemma for the partisans whose own families were affected, it was still felt necessary to do everything possible to rid their lands of the invader. It wasn't until 1947 that the chief perpetrators were finally brought to justice for what was rightly regarded as war crimes.

Actually, partisan activity in the Balkans, especially in Yugoslavia, where the mountains gave refuge to the guerrilas can rightly be compared with Poland and Russia where it was the forests that aided the resistance. But the toll of human life was frightful. It is estimated that about a million and a half Yugoslavs were killed during the occupation, and in Greece some 50,000 resistance fighters were killed together with about 70,000 civilians who were murdered in reprisals. Perhaps most pitiful of all were the 60,000 Jews who were sent to their deaths in the extermination camps, and the quarter of a million or so people who died from privation and hunger (Gilbert, 1989, p.746).

Norway and Denmark fared rather better under the Nazis. This was especially so in the case of Denmark which for most of the occupation enjoyed favoured nation status, possibly because in the Nazi racial hierarchy Danes were considered to be almost kith and kin. But when they began to play up from 1943 onwards, they too merited harsh treatment, though nothing like that meted out in the East. No doubt Germany's declining fortunes had something to do with this. Even German's erstwhile ally, Italy, was not spared once she had defected to the Anglo-American forces in the autumn of 1943. The country was occupied by German troops, and partisan groups were treated unmercifully. In some areas not even the Italian military escaped, as in the Dodecanese.

In some ways the situation in Western Europe presents us with a somewhat ambiguous situation which even so many years afterwards is still difficult to interpret. Belgium, and especially France, are still rife with questionings and recriminations. To a greater or lesser degree every occupied state collaborated with the conqueror. In fact most had their own embyronic Nazi parties which – in the main – welcomed a German victory. Complementarily, many of these states were also notable for their resistance movements which were often most active where the occupying power was particularly repressive – a response which is not as obvious as it seems, given the ruthless, incommesurate reprisals which inevitably followed. Holland is a good example of a divided nation. On the one hand, it had a reasonably healthy National Socialist party and supplied some 17,000 recruits for the Waffen SS, besides another 12,000 or so that took up highly suspect security and police work. On the other hand, Holland had her patriots. There was a well-organized resistance and flourishing underground press. It is estimated that approaching a quarter of a million civilians died as a result of the occupation – a very high proportion of her relatively small population. Furthermore, it should be remembered that as a result of the deportations only about a quarter of her 140,000 Jewish population survived.

One of the most notorious atrocities committed by the Germans in the West was at Oradour-sur- Glane in France in June 1944. The attack on Oradour was one of many 'actions' undertaken against resistance activity in the immediate aftermath of the D-Day landings the previous month. The advent of,the Allied Armies was a signal for the French resistance to rise against their oppressors – something which would divert German troops from reinforcing the northern coastal units who were frantically trying to forestall the Allied advance. Actually, the French resistance had begun operations prematurely in anticipation of the Second Front, and had already lost many of their recruits to actions by both German troops and members of the French collaborationist movement, the Milice. In one action involving five hundred resistants, one hundred and fifty were killed in a battle with German mountain troops who then murdered all the wounded. they could find (Mountfield 1979). In another series of skirmishes, often against overwhelming odds, at Vercors, some two thousand resistants died, also in July.

The Oradour massacre is one of the best documented of such incidents, except that in this case there is no firm evidence that the village harboured any partisans. It was carried out by one of the best known of the Waffen SS units, the Das Reich Panzer division which was on its way north to join other German forces which were doing their best to stem the Allied tide. They had already suffered the worrisome pinpricks of resistance activity, and when this inoffensive village came under suspicion, they decided to set an example. It was really an act of desperation. The Germans were losing the war on all fronts. In the previous year 1943-44, they had lost forty-one 'divisions in Russia alone, and these were precious units that could never be replaced. It was against this background that the vicious attack on the defenceless community at Oradour took place.

Massacre was not new to the Das Reich division. Some of its units had already been involved in the massacre of Jews and partisans (they were conveniently seen in synonymous terms for extermination purposes) in Russia in the heady days of conquest. It had been reformed in 1942, and by then comprised not only Germans but also an appreciable contingent of Hungarians, Romanians and Alsatians. After further service in Russia in 1943, it had been brought back to Southern France for R&R (rest and recuperation) in anticipation of an Allied invasion. By this time many of its number – especially the Alsatians – were young recruits who had served in the SS for only six months or so (Hastings 1981). Most of its NCOs and officers were seasoned professionals, and it was commanded by the rapidly promoted General Hanz Lammerding who already had a reputation for ruthlessness in his dealings with enemy partisans.

The division was frustratingly hampered by resistance activity on its way north, and during a detour through the town of Tulle, the order was given that partisans and their accomplices would pay dearly for the injuries they had inflicted. So the Germans left ninety-nine bodies of hostages hanging from lamp-posts and balconies in the town. In the post-war trials, members of the execution units saw this merely as an 'incident' – a distraction before their main operations began.

The Allied landings were only a few days old, and the division was urgently needed to reinforce the units that were vainly trying to prevent the Allies from bursting out of the beachheads. Nevertheless, Lammerding took the view that the partisans must be taught a very painful lesson. On the afternoon of the 10th June, the SS arrived at Oradour. Everyone was herded into the square, with women and children separated from the men and boys. No one was intended to escape. Machine guns were set up and the executioners were heard laughing and joking as they prepared for their afternoon's work. The men and boys were shot first, and then the buildings housing the women and children were set alight, and they too were either · burned or shot. Soldiers even wandered among the bodies despatching the wounded and the dying. In all 652 were murdered and just ten escaped by simulating death. The killers seemed to have had no qualms about their grisly work.

Only twenty SS men of the original detachment were ever brought to trial. Just two were executed, and eighteen had their life sentences commuted to between five to twelve years. The detachment commander, Otto Dickmann, was killed a few days later in Normandy. Lammerding was sentenced to death in absentia; he had escaped to the Allied Zone, and soon no one was looking for him. There was never any *physical* proof that he gave the orders, no one saw him actually pull a trigger. He was not extradited, but eventually settled in Germany where he became a prosperous business man. He died in 1971.

However, nothing the Germans and their allies did in Western Europe, including Scandinavia, or even in the Balkans, compares with the ravages committed in Poland and Russia. Before the rationalization of the extermination programme at Auschwitz and elsewhere, it is estimated that about a million Jews had already been killed by the Wehrmacht, the Waffen SS, and particularly the specially constituted Einsatzgruppen composed of SS/SD and police personnel. Normally an Einsatzgruppe comprised about a thousand men including support staff. At the opening of the Russian campaign in 1941 there were four such units which were instructed to take all necessary punitive measures against the subject population. This included orders to put to death 'all racially and politically undesirable elements'. Some trouble was taken to guard thir intentions, and sometimes orders were couched in far from explicit terms, but at the later Nuremberg trials when all too few of those involved were present, it became clear that the sub-text was simply to kill anyone who was likely to give trouble.

The Einsatzgrappen were willingly aided by local militia especially in Lithuania and the Ukraine where there was considerable anti-semitic feeling suitably supplemented, of course, by a desire to ingratiate themselves with the conquerors. The units kept meticulous records about their extermination programme which took place on a massive scale and was completed with unrelenting efficiency. In November and December 1941 alone Einsatzgruppen A, B and C had executed over 370,000 people; and in just two days in September 1941, reports show that 33,771 people, mainly Jews, were killed in Kiev. Individual reports confirm the frightening indifference that the SS had to mass murder, SS General Stalecker (Einsatzgruppe A) apologized for killing only 42,000 Jews out of a possible 170,000 in one area because too many were wanted by the Nazi slave labour agencies for urgent work. The winter frosts were also said to have inhibited their lethal activity. With the advent of the spring, however, commanders were able to report that they were meeting, if not exceeding, their targets. Probably by the end of 1942, the final toll was in the region of a million executions mainly by shooting. And this was before the murder machinery of the gas chambers was fully operational.

What cannot be ignored is the obvious relish with which the SS/SD (security service) went about their work. There was a cold insensitivity to the sufferings of others that can be considered psychopathological. And it wasn't just a 'man-thing'; SS women in the camps could be just as brutal. Does this mean that just about anyone can be indoctrinated to do this sort of thing? How can there be sufficient resonance unless we are all actually or potentially, in some sense, evil? Indeed, how can we possibly explain evil of this kind?

Can we go along with psychotherapist Carl Jung (1993) when he speaks of 'Wotanic fury' as an 'archetypal constellation' that has become an historical reality? But an expression such as 'Wotanic fury' is not an explanation; it is not even an adequate description. Yet this sort of approach is not untypical. Jung, who wrote extensively – though inconsistently – on the subject of evil, speaks of the Nazi system as a 'regression of psychic energy to primitive levels of the collective unconscious (which) constellates a compensatory archetypal system' (p.13) – in other words, a reversion to the past. The darker side of human nature Jung euphemistically termed 'the shadow', and in repressive systems (which for Jung meant Nazi Germany-and Soviet Russia) he spoke of 'collective shadows' finding a 'secure playground', and further suggested that under conditions of 'psychological inflation' primitive archetypes are given full rein.

If we can ignore – or re-interpret – the neologistic verbiage, Jung is saying that fanatical ideologies are in some sense demonic because in their identification with archetypal images (in Nazism the nonsense of purported Aryan origins combined with fanciful Teutonic myths), individual accountability and moral consciousness are destroyed. This simply tells us that people are psychologically malleable and susceptible to influences and ideas. But why *these* ideas? Again, we are back to the question of resonance. It may well be argued that evil is a theological concept which has no place in a scientifically-oriented society, and cannot – or should not – be applied to social systems. But what was Nazism if it wasn't a form of perverted religious ideology?

SECTION 3

i) CRIME AND PUNISHMENT: CRITICAL AND REALIST APPRECIATIONS

There is in modern critical criminology a reaction against what postmodernists term 'meta narratives i.e. those overarching, all-inclusive explanatory systems such as we find in political, religious and science-based ideologies. Analogously one might consider traditional ideas/agendas about crime and punishment under a similar heading. Consequently – so the argument goes – those who are concerned with such issues should be prepared to abandon the idea of 'ultimate truth', and 'wage war on totality.... (and) activate the differences' (Lyotard, 1984, pp.81-2). It is said that as criminology as a discipline is so obviously fragmented, we should take this as a cue to discard conservative orthodoxies.

In practice, this means breaking down the discipline into areas of special concern such as race, feminism, homosexuality and the like, and examining each on its merits. This is the typically relative, interactionist approach beloved of post modernists." We are enjoined to be 'reflexive' and therefore sensitive to political conditions and institutional contexts, and abjure any kind of unwarranted essentialism.

From a (right) Realist perspective these views are both mistaken and dangerous. Current understanding of crime and criminals is admittedly limited, and academic appreciations are certainly fragmented. But knowledge – certainly scientific and technical knowledge – must be cumulative. Criminology has to centre on the problem of social order, and must therefore be primarily concerned with crime *control*. Realist theorists are not unaware of the many participating factors such as poverty and poor education which underlie much crime, but somewhat like Behaviourist psychologists – they feel that they must deal with the symptoms rather than the causes which in many cases do not admit of specific identification. So where does criminology go from here? Some theorists insist that it is not really a separate discipline at all, but simply one aspect or application of sociology. Those of the critical school, on the other hand, suggest that we need to stop debating about definitions of criminology, and about exactly where it should be located in the disciplinary spectrum. Instead, they argue, we should concentrate our attention on the structural relations which exist in post-industrial society, and address what they term the 'hierarchies of oppression' (classism, sexism, racism, etc.) which they see as contributing to deviant behaviour. It is their view that it is those who are economically marginalized who are most exposed to the 'processes of criminalization'. This lightly-disguised class-based Marxism has now been joined by neo-colonialism and patriarchy, not to mention heterosexism as the 'true' bases of crime. It would thus appear that crime has a whole range of new causal antecedents.

What is yet more serious for the criminal justice fraternity are those theorists who argue that the whole idea of 'crime' needs to be completely re-conceptualized. They call for partial decriminalization, less recourse to law, as well as a system (if it can be a system) of radical non-intervention regarding certain unspecified crimes (presumably drug offences among others). In short, they advocate a far-reaching overhaul of the whole legal machinery. Indeed, they go as far as suggesting that we abandon the concepts of 'deviance' and even 'behaviour', and instead adopt a 'situation-oriented' (i.e. interactive) approach. This implies, of course, a thorough-going relativism in which all meaningful standards are not only questioned but actually ignored. The implication is that a whole host of crimes could be effectively 'designed out' by a process of re-designation.

The most radical theorists such as Willem de Haan seriously suggest that instead of the concept of crime we should think about 'diverse troubles' (e.g. conflicts, harms, damage, accidents, etc.), and break with the nexus of crime control, punishment and imprisonment. As an alternative – so it is argued – we should think of unspecified national, innovative and constructive 'redress-based mechanisms' for resolving conflicts (de Haan, 1991). This sounds more like an undelineated policy for the resolving of political disputes rather than a blueprint for crime control. Such writers are to be applauded for wanting to shift the emphasis away from some of the injustices which arise in connection with petty crime to the less obvious injustice of society's failure to deal adequately with white-collar crime. They are saying, in effect, that it is mainly the poor and the disadvantaged who tend to be criminalized, while those who commit high profile offences may either go undetected or, if not, can often afford expensive 'silks' 'to represent them. There is, of course, much in the argument, but it is rather simplistic and very far from being the whole truth.

That there are injustices, few would dispute. But this is a far cry from advocating the abolition of prison or even the entire penal system. Yet are these – as abolitionists contend – more rational ways of dealing with crime? Abolitionism as a 'cause' developed in relatively small states in Scandinavia where crime was inherently more manageable than in large crime-ridden countries such as the USA. It was inspired by those whose primary aim was to relax the prison system, and was looking to ways in which punishment – if it was to continue – could be 'humanized'. Its philosophy is encapsulated in the work of social theorist, Michel Foucault who, probably influenced by his own experience as an overt homosexual, maintained that punishment was just one more way in which the state demonstrated its power and domination over the individual.

Absolutionists see crime control rather than crime itself as the real problem. They speak of the 'crime myth' and, unsurprisingly, try to divert our attention to the much more serious crimes of capitalist economies (whether state or privately controlled) and nation states. (For example, should the main directors of the tobacco industry be brought to book for an unheeding policy of mass manslaughter?). But is *their* problem really a semantic one? They speak of 'conflicts' and 'unfortunate events' which should be taken seriously though not as 'crimes', and which can be remedied by various forms of social disapproval. Punishment is thus seen as an expression of 'social negativity'.

What can all this possibly mean? Are we simply playing with words? The truth is that this highly questionable perspective stems from a particular idealist school within sociology which insists that crime is a social construction. However, insofar as 'infringements'. exist these should be subject to dialogue and 'redress', the actual details of which remain frustratingly unclear. In practice, this apparently means treating crime as a kind of disease. So drug problems become mental health problems, violence is a form of social pathology, property crime is a matter for the economy, and so on. In other words, crime is simply being redefined,- but to what end? The naive underlying assumption is that people are certainly improvable, and that human society is therefore potentially much better than its performance to date. All one needs to do is to tinker a little with the social machinery and introduce a new vocabulary: deciminalization, depenalization, destigmatization, etc., and all will be well.

No one is suggesting that the present system of conviction and punishment is perfect, or that there is no room for improvement, but these ideas of some critical criminologists, however well-intentioned, are – on the most generous assessment – totally unrealistic. And many of those who actually work within the criminal justice system regard such avant-garde ideas as patently ridiculous. They see what is sometimes termed the liberal establishment as a repository of unwelcome and unworkable ideas – hardly schemes because they are rarely worked · out. Those who see themselves as 'realist' criminologists are unconvinced by specious arguments that crime is actually on the decline, and that the apparent increase in crime figures is due almost entirely to greater reportage. In fact, there has been a twelve-fold increase in crime generally in the past fifty years – and this certainly cannot be dismissed as statistical error.

Furthermore, as prison medical officer, Theodore Dalryimple, has argued, we cannot by any kind of theoretical manipulation turn the criminal into the victim. It is generally acknowledged, as we have already noted, that many criminals come from disadvantaged backgrounds, but, as we have also seen especially in relation to murder, this is by no means.always the case. Instrumentally, many criminals have quickly assimilated some of this 'new thinking' and now present themselves via their probation officers, social workers and lawyers as the unfortunate victims of society rather than scoundrels and lawbreakers. Even the police are influenced by such ideas especially in relation to minor crime such as, say, soliciting and vandalism. There is little doubt that punishment, correctly and adequately applied, *does* act as a deterrent.(note how many cars slow down when drivers detect a speed trap). Studies of such widely divergent phenomena as draft evasion in the USA and the reduction of drug trafficing in Malaysia have shown that deterrence can work. If criminals are *sure* of punishment, and do not entertain the prospect of undeserved leniency, the criminal justice system might be better served.

Perhaps we need to spend less time theorizing about the causes of crime and concentrate rather on the realities and pragmatics of crime and criminality. John Q. Wilson maintains that the swift processing of the law and the near certainty of incarceration (and in some cases capital punishment) would ensure welcome social control *and* intimidate potential offenders (Wilson 1983).

ii) EXPLANATION AND EXCULPATION I

I have often said to students: suppose I suddenly stopped my lecture, stepped down from the rostrum, and inexplicably began to assault one of them. There would be understandable astonishment. Then having been wrestled to the floor I will have gained some measure of composure and muttered a few apologies. But there would be innumerable questions. What on earth made him do that? Is he ill or something? Should we report it? In short, a need for a convincing explanation. The point I am trying to make here is that when the questions are asked, answers can always be found. Nature abhors a cognitive vacuum. So there will always be some explanation that will *seem* to account for this bizarre behaviour: he's had an argument with his wife; he's had an accident in his car; his shares have taken a fall; he hasn't got enough seratonin, perhaps he has a low sperm count, etc. etc.

Exculpatory 'explanations' are the order of the day; the question is, are they plausible? It is part of social mythology that minor criminals of yesteryear, when their collars were felt, were supposed to accept their arrests without protest, and with 'Fair cop, guv' resignation. This now seems to have given way – especially in major cases.- to the mobilization of a whole battery of exculpatory arguments to account for their misdemeanors which can be supplied to order by court-wise silks and their academic acolytes. The medical and social sciences have found all sorts of convenient reasons why criminals should be treated as special cases. Often the arguments are strongly deterministic, inasmuch as it is suggested that given all the variables it is hardly surprising that this accused person did what he/she did. (Isn't it interesting that similar deterministic arguments are not used to account for achievement, bravery, altruism, genius and the like).

Nowhere is this more evident than in cases of murder. But then, murder is not-just murder. There are moral gradations.

Perhaps the legal system should differentiate more categorically between different kinds of murder. Serial killing and child killing apart, there is probably nothing more heinous than the murder of one's parents and/or family. There are a number of very disturbing cases on record. The brothers, Lyle and Erik Menendez, who killed their parents in 1989 in the hope of inheriting a $14 million fortune. Their defence that they were protecting themselves from sexual abuse strikes many as being the last and malicious recourse of two thoroughly unworthy individuals. A similar defence was vainly offered by Ronald de Feo who shot his entire family in Long Island in 1974. This included his parents, two sisters and two brothers. The twenty-three year old had a history of unspecified psychiatric problems and drug-taking. His counsel's insanity defence was that his client had paranoid delusions that his family were out to kill him. Inexplicably, he was found guilty on six counts of *second*-degree murder and given concurrent sentences of twenty-five years for each. At another time in another place, it might well have been a death sentence.

We might consider two further cases of matricide-patricide committed for very similar motives. Miles Giffard, was the twenty-seven year old son of a reasonably well-to-do solicitor living near the coast in Cornwall. He was personable and athletic (he was a promising County cricketer), and had become involved with a girl in London of whom his parents disapproved. He wanted money to go to London to see her, but they objected. There was a serious altercation, and the young Giffard battered his sixty-two year old father to death, and then killed his mother. He then wheeled their bodies to the cliff top and tipped them over so that when they were found on the rocks below, it would look as though they had both fallen accidentally to their deaths. He then nonchalantly took off for London and spent the time until his arrest with his girl-friend.

The evidence had clearly pointed to murder, and when Giffard was arrested, he freely admitted what he had done. At his trial at Bodmin Assizes, much was made by the defence that he had been bullied by a somewhat arrogant father, 'facts' which need clearly to be specified. He apparently had an unhappy time at boarding school – not an unknown phenomenon – and certainly did not flourish at Public School, and was accused of idleness and lack of concentration. Yet he passed the School Certificate, and when called up he served four years in the Navy without incident. Once demobilized, he lapsed into former habits. He stole from his parents and lied to them about passing his law exams in London. What seems evident is that at twenty-seven the young man could have left home at any time, but was content to benefit from his parents care and generosity (his father had made him an allowance, much of which was spent on drink). The murder appears to have been the petulant and vicious response of someone who at that moment could not get what they wanted. (And did he *have* to murder his mother?) Furthermore, his actions after the crime, give little indication of remorse. It can surely be no excuse for such a crime that it was 'caused' by deep frustration. Obviously, the jury didn't think. so; Giffard was found guilty and hanged in February 1953.

In a more recent case which unaccountably took five years to settle, Eddie Charles was found guilty of triple murder in California in the 1990s. As a relatively impecunious garage mechanic he was unable to keep up with what he perceived to be the 'needs' of his glamorous girlfriend. She was a model and scenic extra in the TV Baywatch series who required wining and dining besides the obligatory breast implants. Consequently, in one way and another, he stole several thousand dollars from his parents, and when they became fully aware of his dishonesty and disloyalty there was a furious argument which resulted in murder. He attacked his brother and put him in the boot of a car. He then killed his parents and put them both on the back seat and after some hours of indecision, set light to the car in which his brother may have been still alive.

Charles was arrested on suspicion, and from prison tried by telephone to persuade his grandfather to take responsibility for the crime. The argument being that he was young and had his whole life before him. Obviously grandfathers were expendable – but this one slammed the phone down. When this ruse failed, he suggested to a fellow inmate that perhaps he could find someone on the outside to murder his grandfather and thus make it look as though some unknown assailant was responsible for *all* the murders. But the inmate saw fit to report the conversation. All credible – if they were credible – moves were now exhausted. Trials and their respective juries came and went, but eventually Charles was found guilty of first degree murder and in 1996 was sentenced to death.

So what should happen to such criminals? This question is inextricably related to two others: should capital punishment be retained or re-introduced? And should the whole issue of prison sentences for such crimes be reviewed?

It is generally accepted that in modern society the primary task of the State is that of security of life. Thomas Hobbes, among others, taught that to maintain human life is intrinsically good, and essential for the other goods we recognize. Therefore, the taking of.life for some private end must be deemed evil. He further argued that the indirect consequence of unrestricted killing was fear; something which made all good activities impossible. Citizens have a right to be protected, and it is not always possible to rely on normative goodwill to achieve this. Consequently, some provision against homicide and its attendant terrors is needed. Only the 'force' of the State can do this (Hobbes, Leviathan, 1651).

The protection of life is a 'primary rule', but there have to be secondary rules which determine how we recognize and identify the *implications* of the primary rule. Furthermore, there have to be secondary rules which determine the *applications* of the primary rule in given circumstances. In other words, we are talking about the interpretation of the law and its subsequent enforcement.

This inevitably raises the question about the nature of enforcement. How should wrongdoers be punished? In modern society, more emphasis has been given to the notion of *reform* than to that of *deterrence*. It is argued by some that deterrence has been tried and failed (proponents often point out that in earlier 'days pickpockets were at work at public hangings when theft itself was a capital crime). Perhaps the *certainty* of punishment – and it is not always *that* certain in crime-ridden society – is more important than the severity of the punishment. And is the extent of deterrence.directly proportional to the severity of punishment? Again, this has to be doubtful where so much crime goes unpunished. Criminals know that the chances of being caught, especially in cases, say, of burglary are minimal. Even in crimes as serious as rape, arrest – *when* it happens – is by no means always followed by conviction. All of which suggests that we need better trained, better led, and more adequately manned police forces.

But do we also need better (i.e. tougher) laws, prosecutors and judges? In very general terms, there are five kinds of legal response to those found guilty of crimes:

i)   admonition followed by some form of subsequent supervision by an agency such as a probation service (those with suspended sentences could come into this category)

ii) admonition plus a specified period of community service

iii) commitment – especially for juvenile defendents
   – to appropriate institutions which have a 'boot camp' or otherwise educational orientation

iv) custodial sentences

v) permanent removal from society either by imprisonment or death.

The first four of these clearly anticipate the return of the criminal to society. This presupposes that there has hopefully been some degree of moral regeneration, although the incidence of recidivism does not leave too much room for optimism. This raises yet again the age-old penological problem as to whether punishment is about reformation or retribution. 'But is this a false dichotomy? In theory, there is no logical reason why it should not be both. Can there be any good reason why, for instance, thugs who attack elderly people and rob them of their savings should not be severely punished as a form of retribution? Indeed, some might well argue that those who cause physical suffering either to people or to animals should suffer physically themselves. Experiments in penology are hardly that innovative, but if as a by-product of disciplined incarceration there is some welcome change of heart, all well and good. Fear of further incarceration will have had a salutary effect.

Murder is a very special category. And sentencing for murder, more than with most other crimes (excepting perhaps rape and terrorism) reflects society's desire for revenge. Few would disagree that it is the most heinous of crimes, and in certain instances, e.g. serial killing, child murder, etc. generates such public outrage that any display of mercy is out of the question. Hence the consistent clamour, even in the UK, for the re-introduction of capital punishment.

Society not only has to be protected from wrongdoers, but its laws must also be vindicated. Kant, considered by many to be the greatest of post-medieval philosophers, argued that 'judicial punishment.... can never be inflicted simply and solely as a means to forward a good, other than itself.... but must at all times be inflicted on (the criminal) for no other reason than because he has acted criminally.... but if justice perishes, then it is no more worthwhile that that man should live upon the earth' (quoted by Benn & Peters, 1959, pp.174-5). Utilitarian theorists tend to argue for a justification for retributive punishment in terms of what brings the greatest happiness – or least harm – to the greatest number. But Kant and other retributivist theorists argue instead that punishment *as a rule* does not exist to further someone's interests or advantage; it is its own justification. All that has to be justified is any *particular application* of the rule. In other words, there must be careful discrimination and consistency at all levels of the legal system.

Judicial acts, especially those as unpleasant as inflicting punishment, require some justification. So the retributivist resorts – quite understandably – to an *ethical* argument and insists that it is morally repugnant that persons should injure others without suffering injury themselves. Punishment is something the guilty *deserve*; in a sense, it is something they owe society. Furthermore, detention of such people can be considered legitimate as a means of social control, and as a policy to ensure some measure of social security. Those who object to such procedures counter that they effectively also punish the innocent (i.e. the dependents and relatives of those convicted), but it also has to be pointed out that it gives some degree of psychological comfort to the dependents and relatives of the victims – a social category which is too often overlooked. To take an extreme case: it may be a poor consolation for the Jewish people to see perpetrators of the Holocaust punished – but it is *something* considering that too many escaped altogether.

As far as actual penalties are concerned, it has to be admitted that crime and punishment are usually incommensurable. There is usually no direct relation between the offence and the penalty, e.g. how can one assess, say, the term of imprisonment for a convicted blackmailer' or an embezzler? Punishment has to be graded on a rough scale, and often there is no clear agreement between judges or magistrates on the degree of severity for any particular crime. The principal exception is capital crime, but even here there are many disturbing anomalies. Should rape, for example, be a Capital crime as it is in some American states (and confusingly not others)? Convicted rapists have been known to spend more years on Death Row than they would have served for the same offence in Britain, and *then been executed*. And what about terrorism? Should this only be seen as a Capital crime where such acts have resulted in a loss of life?

Just as pertinent is the question of treason and spying. Should they only be a Capital crime in wartime? (In wartime Britain, spies were given summary justice; those who refused to be 'turned' were quickly hanged). Yet traitors such as Kim Philby divulged information which certainly resulted in several deaths, as did also the long undetected activities of Aldrich Ames in the USA. Both betrayed their countrymen to a *potential*, not an actual enemy. And what of the Rosenbergs who were involved in a spy ring which was certainly instrumental in hastening the Soviet efforts to produce murder weapons. They were convicted and executed in peacetime because they increased a potential threat to the USA which may or may not have been actualized. Yet to be fair to the West, it should be said that we shall probably never know how many people were put to death by the NKVD/KGB for similar offences.

Terrorism, treason and spying, by implication, raise the vexed issue of torture. Can torture ever be justified? Although the question is much debated by Human Rights activists, it would seem that a case can be made for torture on utilitarian grounds. If we suppose that in a bomb threat situation many lives will be lost unless a captured terrorist can be made to say where it is and when it is timed to explode. On the other hand, a quite different view should be taken of gratuitous torture which sometimes accompanies rape and murder. Where this horrendous combination of crimes – rape, torture and murder – does take place, as it has in some of the worst cases of serial homicide, how can the punishment be made to fit the crime? Or when the scale of murder is such that it defies all attempts to calculate the degree of culpability as in, say, the crimes of Marcel Petiot in France, Andrei Chikatilo in Russia, the Wests in Britain, or of Ed Gein in the USA, again how does even the execution of the perpetrator begin to make up for the monumentality of the offences?

Any consideration of sentencing almost inevitably calls yet again for some discussion of the problem of 'mental instability'. The key issue here is, of course, exactly what the term means. How can it be defined and how can it be discerned? And *if* it has any meaning at all, to what extent should allowance be made for it, particularly where violent crime is concerned? It is noteworthy that there is now at the University of Leeds a Centre for Criminal Justice Studies. The intention is to conduct research into the relationship between mental health problems and crime. It is based in the Department of Law, and has been set up to promote 'a broader social and political perspective of crime'. In short, it is an attempt to widen the whole area of criminological studies. At the moment though, their work is mainly concerned with minor offences which are thought to result from some kind of 'mental disorder', but the implication is clear that 'mental disorder'-is an exculpatory factor. Justice is thus thought to be served if this factor is given due consideration.

What must be asked, however, is this: let us suppose that some vaguely defined form of mental illness or imbalance is held to account for the commission of the crime(s), must it also account for the degree or form of punishment? And how easy is it to make mistakes? It is often said by those who are opposed to capital punishment that it is better that ten guilty men should go free than that one innocent man should suffer. But an equally good case could be made that if necessary it would be better for one innocent man to die than that the Petiots, Chikatilos, Wests and Geins, etc. of this world (the total of whose victims can be counted in the hundreds) should go free.

It has already been argued that 'mental disorder' (including psychopaths, sociopaths, etc.) is not the happiest of diagnoses. What, for example, are we to make of Peter Sutcliffe, the Yorkshire Ripper, a murderer of thirteen women, who is at present ensconsed in Broadmoor mischievously playing off one female admirer against another. He corresponds with several, and one was reported as being near suicidal when she found that she was only one of many. It would appear if there is any 'mental disorder' anywhere it is to be found in women who fawn on a mass killer, than in Sutcliffe himself.

And how often is the 'mental disorder' dimension exploited? In a recent case in the North East of England, a young woman was found stabbed to death in her house. She had been married only days before to a man nearly twice her age, although they had lived together for some time before this, much to the disapproval of her parents. The husband was missing, but he had had the forethought to phone the police and tell them that he was making for the 600ft high cliffs on the coast with the intention of killing himself. The police hastened to the scene, located the man and 'persuaded' him not to jump. Attempted suicide is associated with 'disturbance of the mind'. Perhaps it was a good move on the husband's part; it should go well with the court when he is tried for murder.

iii) EXPLANATION AND EXCULPATION II

Making the punishment fit the crime has always been something of a problem. After all, the two are hardly commensurable. Though perhaps in the case of murder, the ancient lex talionis would seem to give us a reasonable guideline. The prescription of an 'eye for an eye' which initially sounds rather brutal, was actually meant to be merciful. The idea was that one *only* took an eye for an eye and nothing more. So in the case of murder it was simply a life for a life.

Though murder comes in different forms, and each must be considered on its merits or otherwise there is no doubt that in the UK, and particularly in the USA, the application of the law can – on the most generous estimate – be considered to be somewhat idiosyncratic. Much of the disparity in sentencing arises from tacit or overt forms of plea-bargaining, or from factors which are regarded as exculpatory. After all, it is the task of the defence to 'do their best for their client', even if this means adopting the most implausible legal strategems. At worst, it can involve what can only be described as ethical prostitution where solicitors/counsel are prepared to defend – for a fee – the patently indefensible (note the attempts to obtain an appeal hearing for multiple murderer Rosemary West, convicted in 1995 for the killing of ten women at her house in Gloucester). Legally, of course, even the most vicious criminals are entitled to a defence, but appeals are another thing. In the USA especially, successions of trials and hearings can drag on for several years even in cases where there is no serious doubt as to the degree of culpability. It is possible for clever lawyers to explore every technicality and legal loophole to obtain concessions for their clients and turn the cases in question (most notably in relation to organized crime) into little more than a farce.

Elliot Leyton cites the case of American serial killer, Aileen Wuornos, who – with the help of her counsel – claimed that her conviction for seven murders was unjust. She insisted that she had been misunderstood. (I'm not a man-hating lesbian who only killed to rob.... This is a downright fabrication and very far from the truth'). Wuornos, had been abandoned by her mother and was homeless at fifteen. She was purportedly ill-treated by an alcoholic grandfather, and had been a prostitute since her early teens. She insisted that she was not a serial killer, 'I killed a series of men, but it was in self-defence.... my only premeditation was to get out and make another dollar' (Leyton, 1997, p.214). But the jury didn't misunderstand; she was sentenced to death in Florida in 1992.

It hardly needs to be said that many people have had difficult, even traumatic childhoods, yet- have not resorted to crime, and certainly not to murder. It is then something of an insult to law abiding people when those who do turn to crime seek to justify their actions in these terms.

The issues of mitigation and idiosyncratic sentencing are frequently seen in combination. Take the more recent case of the Archibald brothers itinerant gypsies (tinkers)?) from Wapseys Wood in Buckinghamshire. John Archibald was convicted of raping a terminally ill woman in a nursing home in February 2000, although his brother, Mark Archibald was acquitted of assault on the same woman for lack of 'reliable' evidence. The woman's husband, a BBC television presenter, said his wife who has Huntington's Disease, a fatal degenerative brain condition, was raped while in a heavily medicated state in front of another wheelchair-bound resident. The woman judge, Mary Mowat, incomprehensibly, sentenced Archibald to a mere three years in prison (effectively, probably only *two* years) for what she admitted was a 'repellent, wicked and disgusting' crime. In mitigation, she said she had taken into account the fact that the offender had an IQ of only 52 and was low in his class at a school for those with learning difficulties. Should this make any difference? Surely society can do without 'this kind of ignorant thug whose brother, needless to say, threatened the poor woman's husband with 'revenge' after the trial. Justice – it seems – is obviously becoming a problem.

Can the Archibalds and people like them be trusted not to re-offend? Should we take an unpopular yet more realistic view and punish the criminal rather than the crime? This sounds harsh, but might it be more effective in the long-term? Of course, we are *all* capable of killing another person, but very few of us actually do.

Graham Young, a self-confessed poisoner was released from Broadmoor Hospital for those considered criminally insane, but even after nine years incarceration, he was not 'cured'. He was not considered violent – but this did not mean that he wasn't dangerous. Once back in society he went to work for a firm making photographic instruments. He was given fairly simple tasks including making the tea. In June 1971, one of his colleagues was suddenly taken ill with what was believed to be peripheral neuritis, and died soon afterwards in hospital. Several other members of staff were also affected by this strange illness which was conveniently attributed to a virus of some kind. Alternatively, some thought that it might be due to the effects of some of the chemicals used in photographic processing. A few months later another employee died, and seemingly staff were impressed by Young's interest in the deaths and his apparent knowledge of such matters. So much so, in fact, that when an investigation was being carried out, he actually asked the doctor if the cause could possibly be thallium poisoning.

The police now began to look into the matter, and on checking Young's records discovered that the twenty-three year old had once been found to have poisoned his step-mother and had tried to poison two other members of the family. On his arrest, he was found to be carrying a lethal dose of thallium and a diary containing names of those he intended to poison. He boasted that he could have killed others, but had magnanimously 'allowed them to live'. It should have been ominous when in earlier years he had been found experimenting by poisoning pet animals.

At his trial in 1972, Young tried in vain to deny everything, but he was convicted and sentenced to life in prison. Not Broadmoor this time, but Parkhurst – the abode of 'normal' prisoners. In 1990, he was found dead in his cell, apparently from a heart attack. It is interesting to ask why if Young was classified as insane as a youth, he was not similarly classified as an adult? Or perhaps the initial diagnosis was wrong or, at least, questionable.

One highly contentious solution – if it is a solution – is that there should be no such thing as an insanity plea. The lines are obviously so fine between what some regard as insane and what is considered normal that the distinction is quite clearly blurred. Furthermore, in practice we are confronted especially in murder trials – with the unseemly wrangling between prosecution and defence 'expert witnesses' who cannot agree on whether their clients are insane or otherwise; whether they know the difference between right and wrong; whether they knew what they were doing at the time of the crime, etc. etc. When 'experts' differ, who can agree? And the whole issue is exacerbated by the question of schools and categories. Do the psychiatrists involved favour neo-Freudian interpretations, or are they Behaviourists or Cognitivists, or do they favour a more humanistic approach? And how much are 'life experiences to be taken into consideration? The 'Black Panther', Donald Neilson, is currently serving three terms of life imprisonment for the murder of three sub-postmasters, and twenty-one years for kidnap and murder of a teenage girl. His defence team · offered a variety of 'reasons' why this one-time soldier who had served during the emergency in Kenya should have become such a violent criminal. He lost his mother when he was eight; he was bullied at school; he missed the excitement and discipline of Army life; after demobilization he was unsuccessful as a small-time builder, etc.... And so it goes on. Take your choice. On any reasonable analysis, these are all pretty lame excuses for multiple murder. But what else could the defence do? They really had nothing 'to work with, so should they even try?

The 'insanity' issue has other, even more contentious, implications. What is to be done with those criminals who are clearly 'possessed' by an apparently incurable obsession to torture-and/or kill? In California in 1969 there was an unsolved series of murders. Couples were either wounded or murdered, sometimes in their cars. Letters – regarded at the time as genuine – were sent to various San Francisco newspaper offices signed by 'the Zodiac'. The person admitted responsibility for the crimes, and offered to give himself up. Either he or another caller, phoned in and insisted that he'd 'got to kill'. Contact was broken, but the letters and threats began again in 1971 and continued until 1974. The writer claimed to have killed thirty-seven times. The police conceded that homicide patterns across the USA indicated that this might well be the case as the locations of the murders when plotted on the map formed a large letter Z. The Zodiac killer was never caught. But it is interesting to speculate what kind of judgement would have been forthcoming at his trial.

A particularly distressing case in England in the 1950s was that of John Straffen. This raised yet again the question of what exactly is meant by 'insane' and 'mentally subnormal', and precisely how such individuals ought to be judged. In societies where murder is a capital crime, should such categories automatically exempt the guilty from the death sentence?

As a youth, John Straffen, an habitual truant and petty thief, was classified as 'mentally subnormal' and sent to a special school. At seventeen he assaulted a young girl, and was arrested, and found to be 'feeble-minded' (i.e. educationally subnormal) having an IQ of only 58, and sent to the appropriate institution. By this time he was already displaying dangerous signs of cruelty by taking pleasure in strangling chickens. This should have been taken as a possible indicator of things to come, although at least one teacher reported that he was rather timid and solitary. Yet the very fact that he had previously been apprehended for fourteen house-breaking offences suggests that he was not that stupid.

After two years at the 'Colony', he was licensed out and was hoping for a full discharge, but he was recalled for theft. In July 1951, a few days after an appointment with the Medical Officer for Bath, Straffen lured a little girl into a field and strangled her. He then went – quite unconcerned – to the cinema. A month later he murdered another small child who only moments before had been seen laughing with him. He was arrested, committed to Reading Assizes, but was found unfit to plead, and sent to Broadmoor. There his mental state obviously improved because, as it later transpired, he had learned to play contract bridge and devised an ingenious method of escape. He was only free for four hours, but it was enough time in which to murder yet another small girl.

His trial took place at Winchester Assizes. It was evident that he felt no remorse, and the arresting officer reported that Straffen had said, 'She's dead, but you can't prove I did it', and laughed. When questioned by one doctor, he said about one murder that he had done it 'to annoy the police.... because he hated them'. From his examination, the Specialist classified Straffen as a *moral* defective who had no more feeling about his crimes than the average person would have about killing a fly. As such, he concluded, Straffen was incurable and would therefore be quite unresponsive to either treatment or punishment.

Straffen, although generally regarded as 'insane', was nevertheless considered responsible under the provisions of the McNaughten Rules and was sentenced to death. But whether he should have been subsequently reprieved is highly arguable. In theory, what were termed 'mentally subnormal' people were those individuals who were regarded as incapable of improvement. Yet this does not appear to be true of Straffen who displayed a certain degree of educability – not to say, cunning in his dealings with the police and the psychiatrists.

And even if by both subjective (psychiatry) and objective (brain scans) tests such a person is shown to be abnormal, surely such a person is too dangerous to have a place in what we optimistically call 'civilised society'?

Degrees of moral obliquity are not always easy to determine. Thus it follows that degrees of legal culpability have to be subject to certain qualifications. But should psychopathy (*not* psychopathology which is not the condition, but *theories* of the condition) however defined – be considered grounds for a plea of diminished responsibility? Some theorists maintain that we should distinguish between *responsibility* i.e.. the extent to which people are accountable for their acts, and *culpability* which refers to the ethical (or, as some would say, wickedness) dimension of those acts. But can these two factors be effectively separated? Similarly – especially in cases of murder – can we confidently regard psychopathy as a 'disease of the mind' rather than a 'character defect'? And to assume that these terms can be precisely defined is a matter of considerable uncertainty. This is highlighted especially in the case of Miles Giffard where experts debated whether his condition was the forerunner or the aftermath of schizophrenia. It is known that what one psychiatrist calls psychopathy may be regarded by a second as schizophrenia, and by a third as a form of hysteria. These are mere diagnostic labels which really have no very precise meaning.

Similar problems are raised by the issue of what are termed exogenous and endogenous causes. In less technical terms, is the individual's state of mind due to external circumstances, and therefore relieved when those circumstances change, or is it due to some constitutional or other inherent condition. But, yet again, we have to ask to what extent these also can be clearly distinguished? If, for example, it is argued that a particular individual commits a particular crime as the result of 'acute depression' (an extreme but well known example would be a mother who kills her child), what have we actually said? Usually people are depressed for a reason: poverty, redundancy, bereavement, or whatever. In other words, social circumstances have psychological effects. It is now common to think of depression as a disease. But whether one can confidently speak of 'depressives' or people with what was once called 'involutional melancholia' as though this was an inherent and presumably ineradical facet of their natures raises all sorts of questions. It implies a thoroughgoing determinism – that such people can be no other than what they are, and who therefore can never be responsible for their actions.

Alternatively, in cases where the 'trade' is convinced that a particular individual can be improved by some form of therapy, what choices have we? Well, we can begin with the therapies which derive from the traditional – one might almost say classic – schools of psychology. The Psychodynamic school, for instance, which derives its basic ideas from Freud and those neo-Freudians whose clinical techniques share certain common features, hold that the key to understanding the human personality is to be found in the unconscious mind. The fundamental pre-supposition is that humans, by their very nature, are a product of a competitive evolutionary process. As such they are at war with a society which commands restraint. Humans are therefore aggressive and self-interested, and the task of socially-ordered entities (nations, states, communities) is to constrain individuals and help them to come to terms with their 'alien' environments. In short, people are at the mercy of their own unknown or undiscovered natures which can only be 'revealed' by the appropriate therapy. In effect, it is another form of determinism.

Psychodynamic theorists distinguish between suppression and repression. They define *suppression* as the conscious control of our unruly natures. It is argued that in this deliberate attempt to suppress our feelings we may give rise to an unwelcome variety of neuroses, perhaps resulting in certain criminal or at least antisocial acts. Suppression is therefore the opposite of expression. The trick is to sublimate any undesirable urges such as aggression in relatively harmless ways. *Repression*, on the other hand, is the unconscious control of desire. It is the inability – or in certain cases the refusal – to recognise certain proclivities, such as, say, sexual deviance. If such a condition is not 'treated', so it is argued, it may result in dangerous psychotic repercussions. Individuality therefore, can only find its safe expression within a recognised social framework. Conduct is acceptable providing it has the imprimatur of the community because uncoordinated self-expression can only lead to personal and social disaster.

The implications are legion. The causal hypotheses are virtually endless. What leads to what? All it takes is an unremembered or unperceived childhood trauma to produce a serial killer! The 'cause' of behaviour patterns is often quite unverifiable, but acceptance of the therapist's 'explanation' may well have beneficial therapeutic effects. Hence the conclusion of many critics that such forms of therapy may help with the symptoms but rarely uncover the cause.

A disturbing modern variant of the Psychodynamic approach is th.·t of 're-birthing' therapy. This is itself another form of 'primal scream' treatment whereby the patient is taken orally through the experience of birth on the assumption that being born is everyone's initial trauma. Obviously, as this is something none of us can recall, it is a prime candidate to bear the responsibility for any and every subsequent behaviour pattern. 'Re-birthing', however, goes an ominous step further. Here candidates may be immersed in water or are garbed in a way that is supposed to simulate containment within the womb. Their 'escape', which is sometimes made purposely difficult, is supposed to represent emergence from the birth canal – a struggle which is encouraged verbally by the ritual attendants.

This procedure which apologists say just involves a breathing technique, besides being frankly idiotic, can actually be dangerous, as one recent death in Colorado by suffocation has shown. It has been used in the USA since 1970 to treat undisciplined children who are said to have been suffering from 'reactive attachment disorder' (RAD), in other words, the supposed inability to form emotional attachments. Actually, the term is used to describe children who are said to be difficult to control. It may be a question of 'show me a symptom, and I'll give it a name'. Once this has happened, a therapy is not far away. Needless to say, it arrived in the UK in 1991, and there now exists a British Rebirth Society.

Much more down to earth is Behavioural Therapy. Yet this too has a deterministic basis. What the Psychodynamic theorists regard as merely the tip of the iceberg – i.e. actual observed behaviour – the Behaviourists see as the only real area of study. They are not principally concerned with the underlying causes of behaviour because these may never actually be known. For example what makes a particular individual a serial killer may be undiscernible even to the person concerned. It is not enough to accept at face value their own admission that they 'enjoy killing', one must ask *why* they do. And this may be as difficult to answer as why someone likes chips and hates cabbage. Behaviourists claim to be scientific in their procedures, and argue that science is not interested in non-examinable phenomena. Therefore they take the view that they are going to deal only with *observed* behaviour, and they do this with moderate success with certain kinds of therapy, for instance, sex therapy and some problems of sexual dysfunction. It isn't that Behaviourists are unconcerned with causes, but they insist that for all practical purposes the symptoms must come first. But the view that behaviour, like that of rats in mazes, is essentially a matter of stimulus and response (i.e. change the stimulus and you will change the response) strikes many of us as just a little too simplistic.

Closely related to Behaviourism is what is commonly known as Learning Theory which is particularly pertinent to the question of criminal behaviour. Learning theorists argue that human behaviour cannot be adequately explained in terms of biological pre-dispositions, but is learned by initiation and inculcation, and not least by imitation. So is this how people become criminals? Is it really all a question of upbringing, environment and peer pressure,or is there -as more psychoanalytically-oriented theorists would argue – rather more to it than this?

Alternatively, there are those who favour Humanistic theories and their therpeutic application. Humanistic theorists (together with their close cousins the Cognitive theorists) have reacted against what they see as the sterility of Behaviourism. Their ideas tend to attract those members of the 'caring professions' (social workers and the like) who, in general, take what they feel is a more compassionate approach to the problem members of the community. Contrary also to the neo-Freudians who tend to concentrate on those 'shadow' aspects of the human personality (to use Carl Jung's favourite term), Humanistic theorists emphasize the more positive features of human behaviour. They dislike thinking of humans in mechanistic terms, and stress instead that humans are intelligent, purposive beings. They disparage too any undue emphasis on the debilitating effects of guilt and failure, and prefer to concentrate rather on the possibilities inherent in human potential. The goal – in the words of their great high-priest, Abraham Maslow – is, or should be, 'self-actualization'. This is a term which even the aficionados find difficult to define at all precisely, though the general idea of achieving one's potential – whatever that is – is reasonably self-evident.

It is clear how such an approach might well appeal to those concerned with theorizing about crime and criminals. It is especially attractive to those who entertain strong convictions about the reformative aspects of penal policy. Though not, needless to say, so much among those who actually deal with crime and criminals. By being prospective rather than retrospective, and telling clients to disregard past failings, and to think positively about the future, they sometimes achieve beneficial results. But they do so by minimizing a sense of guilt which may be the necessary precursor to true reform – if, indeed, that is possible.

As far as the degree of guilt and punishment are concerned, one must always try to distinguish between *extenuating* and *exonerating* circumstances. Some commentators would also like to include the notion of 'irresistible impulses', but there is always the danger of thinking of almost any impulse that was obviously – and criminally – not resisted as demonstrably irresistible. Irresistibility implies determinism, and determinism makes nonsense of justice and responsibility. It is little more than a counsel of despair, yet it has to be admitted that in some cases there may be no other option. To show the causes of behaviour is not to deny that people are free agents. 'Causes' however defined or identified – may be seen as the necessary but not the sufficient explanations for any form of behaviour. Causal exculpability is not the same as causal unavoidability.

Punishment may be inflicted not out of revenge or anger, but out of a dispassionate sense of justice. Some will inevitably ask if it is not better to forgive and restore the offender. But it must be pointed out that those who inflict judicial punishment are rarely those whose duty or inclination is to forgive. Whether the offender is to be punished or not, and to what degree, is normally decided by those who are not personally affected by the offence. Therefore it is not necessarily a virtue for them to forgive the offender. The point – or onus – of forgiveness lies with those who have been wronged. In fact it is an effrontry for those who are not victims of an offence to forgive – or *say* they forgive – harm done to others. The impartial functionaries of the justice system presumably have nothing to forgive. Forgiveness does not necessarily mean that the offender does not deserve punishment. Indeed, it has often been argued that genuinely penitent offenders will accept punishment as a form of psychological absolution – a way of atonement for their crimes.

EXCURSUS: THE BARRY GEORGE CASE

The confusion in diagnostic thinking can well be seen in the (2000) case of Barry George who was convicted of the murder (some might argue clinical assassination) of BBC presenter, Jill Dando. Although both identification and forensic evidence were weak, George an undoubted obsessive who had a previous conviction for attempted rape and assault was seen as the most likely prospect.

At the time there was a widespread view, especially among crime journalists including highly respected Max Hastings, that the verdict, based almost entirely on circumstantial evidence, was unsafe. There was compelling evidence – revealed only after the trial – that mentally George was clearly below par. Investigation showed that he was a fantasist and poseur – he liked to pretend, among other things, that he was or had been a member of the Special Forces. His medical history also indicated a capacity for violence. He may also have been something of a misogynist – certainly his contacts with women (most notably his relationship with his estranged wife) did not show him in the best light. He was a celebrity buff who assumed various identities, and who is thought to have stalked numerous women, sometimes clad in the 'classic rapist's kit', balaclava, combat fatigues and a commando knife. But was he also a murderer?

How, then, should he be classified? Needless to say, herein lies the confusion. Some psychiatric reports purport to show that George is a 'deeply dishonest egoist' who would show little shame or remorse for a cold-blooded killing. In short, he has a 'psychopathic personality' disorder, a person of reasonable intelligence with an incapacity for love. It then transpired that, he might have two personality disorders – and possibly three or even four. His obvious attention-seeking tendencies earned him the further diagnosis of possessing a 'histrionic personality disorder'. Added to this, his aggressive behaviour towards women, branded him as someone with a 'narcissistic personality disorder', while his mistrust of others clearly indicated that he had a 'paranoid personality disorder'. Moreoever, some 'experts' believed that his awareness of such diagnoses allowed him to adopt an unconvincing 'sick role' persona. And may have exaggerated the symptoms of epilepsy for which he had been treated, while implicitly blaming the medication for his 'rages'.

Yet another forensic psychologist, Dr. Keith Ashcroft at the University of Edinburgh, is reported as having likened George's symptoms to those characteristic of erotomania or De Clerambault Syndrome, the condition where a person erroneously believes that he/she is loved by another. The object of this admiration or adoration − needless to say − is usually quite unaware of the situation. The condition may take intense forms if the attention (messages, gifts, etc.) are unrequited. On the other hand, it may exist as little more than a harmless' fantasy (The actor Peter-Sellers is said to have harboured such thoughts about Princess Margaret).

David Canter, Professor of Psychology at the University of Liverpool, has rounded on his fellow experts for their convenient use of 'pseudo-medical terms' in this case, and has also politely dismissed the further assertion that George suffers from Asperger's Syndrome (a mild form of autism).

It is all probably a case of nature abhoring a cognitive vacuum. Where no really convincing explanation is forthcoming, any half-decent hypothesis will do. At least this has been the view of many since George was cleared after a re-trial (2008). This is not to suspect an official 'fit-up' by the police, but it does suggest that they were placed in an invidious position when after a whole year since the murder of such a high-profile personality, they had still not come up with a likely suspect. Desperation of this kind − as the George case exemplified − has its own real dangers. Now their situation has become almost impossible. They have to find a murderer who − for them − probably doesn't exist.

iv) EXPLANATION AND EXCULPATION III
DRUGS, BRAIN DAMAGE AND THE GENETIC FACTOR

In the Social Sciences – of which Criminology may be said to be a sub-genre the whole question of Research Methodology is a much-debated issue. Among the possible bases of confusion is the failure often to distinguish between:

i) Causality i.e. A leads to B

ii) Concomitance i.e. A accompanies B – while both may be related to further antecedent factors

iii) Correlation i.e. A in terms of B

iv Coincidence i.e. where A and B despite some initial impressions – are actually unrelated

Nowhere is this confusion more evident in the study of crime than in the assumed relationship between bio-chemical factors and various forms of criminal behaviour. Are these causally linked, or is the connection – though not coincidental – merely concomitant? To exemplify the point, we could take the case of Dion Sanders, a troublesome individual from childhood, who led a generally feckless existence, and who eventually murdered his grandparents who had brought him up, because they refused to give him money for drugs. With no credible defence for his actions, his lawyers resorted to a bio-chemical deficiency gambit – he was discovered to have a low seratonin level which just *may* have affected his ability to control his violent behaviour. Implausible as it may -seem, it saved him from the death penalty and secured him prison for life in Ohio with no possibility of parole.

One suspects that it would make just as much sense to correlate a tendency to violence with diminutive stature. Sanders certainly falls into this category, as do so many violent individuals in the past. Could cruelty and callousness be some kind of over compensation for being small? Preposterous as it may seem, such a thesis could have a certain cogency in the case of *some* personalities. Napoleon was small, so was Robespierre, the instrument of the revolutionary Terror in France. Alexander the Great was also small – when after the conquest of Persia, he sat on the Great King's Throne, his feet didn't touch the ground. And what of one of the most murderous of Stalin's henchmen? It did not pay to ridicule Comrade Yetzov even though his overcoat touched his feet. Yes, implausible as it is, one *could* make a case.

But the bio-chemical argument can be employed both ways. It may not be just a question of deficiency; indeed, according to some experts, there are individuals who have too much of a good thing. In the 1980s in Connecticut there was a series of murders of young women which was attributed to an over-abundance of the male hormone, testosterone. A young man, Michael Ross, was eventually convicted of raping and strangling eight young women and leaving their bodies to rot in the woods. There was no question of his guilt; he made a full confession and helped the police to locate his victims. Needless to say, there can be no proven *causal* connection between testosterone levels and serial murder (how many non-murderers also have such levels?), and this discovery did not save Ross from multiple death penalties. Yet it did enhance the prejudiced view that all men are violent, although it is an incontrovertible fact that most murders are committed by men. Ergo, the now growing practice of chemical castration which is intended to help men to govern their wilder sexual impulses. But does this mean that evil is to be equated with hormonal imbalance?

Equally suspect in causal terms is the whole question of brain damage. Can brain trauma, whether as the result of some congenital or otherwise neuropathic condition, actually be the primary cause of violent behaviour? Or can brain damage attributable to injuries sustained.as the result of parental beatings – a 'cause' very close to the hearts of desperate defence lawyers – really account for a defendant's ungovernable cruelty, sadism or whatever? Of course, in the case of murder, it is true that it is not the gun or the knife but the *brain* that kills. It is a mental decision. But to show – as. brain scans often do' – some physical deformity in the brain geometry of violent persons does not establish a *causal* connection between a physical state and particular behaviours, violent or otherwise. It merely indicates that there is a plausible *correlation* between two factors.

We could look at one or two actual cases to illustrate this point. In 1998 in Denver, Colorado, an attractive twenty-four year old woman was attacked by a powerful (300 lb) intruder who, according to his own confession, was intent only on robbery. There was a frantic struggle, but eventually he was able to tie the woman up before he left the house. It all might have ended there, but for reasons which neither he not anyone else is able satisfactorily to explain, he returned and savagely cut and stabbed the woman to death. Whether Donta Page's primary motive was sexual or simply to prevent identification is not absolutely certain. But the murder of Peyton Tuthill led to a critical debate as to whether or not he merited the death penalty.

Page's defence team pulled out all the stops. Expert forensic psychiatrists testified on both sides. It transpired that Page had been systematically abused as a child, and that this had resulted in brain dysfunction. Eventually, he was given the benefit of the doubt, and was sentenced to life without the possibility of parole. Yet the (un)perceived anomaly here is that all the special pleading did not mitigate his responsibility for the act – a point forcibly made by a prosecution expert, Dr. Dan Martell. Page was still guilty of an heinous crime. But a brain scan was able to save him from death.

Does this make sense? Surely if brain damage is to be seen as exculpatory, it *is* exculpatory. The person is not really responsible for his action. In this case the judgement suggests that he was not quite responsible, or not entirely responsible. If brain damage is going to be invoked, then how much *is* it going to account for? How can it possibly be quantified? And just how is this going to be assessed in penal terms?

It is all very well to argue, as America's Professor Jonathan Pincus does, that damage to the frontal lobe of the brain can be related – whatever that means – to violent behaviour. Or at least, that it can be detected in persons who have exhibited violent behaviour. This line of argument is also supported by Professor Adrian Raine, another eminent neuroscientist. From his extensive studies he maintains – more guardedly – that murderers are very likely to have suffered from frontal lobe damage which has probably been caused by physical abuse in childhood. But this is very different from asserting that by examining the scans we can know what is going on in the brain. Or, indeed, that we can predict with any reasonable accuracy how this or that person will act in future. Even if we could anticipate violent behaviour, there is no way of knowing what form it will take.

A further related argument not unusually advanced by defence lawyers in certain cases lays stress on the adverse environmental conditions in which the accused was raised. Colourful court annals, provide us with a succession of schizophrenic mothers and alcoholic/drug dependent, sadistic fathers (or preferably step-fathers) who are held to be the real criminals. But interesting as all this is as background information it should not detract from where the ultimate responsibility lies. Lack of love in childhood does not explain violence – indeed there are many cases on record where violence has followed excessive indulgence. And others where excessive violence has followed unexceptional childhood. Witness the recent (2004) confession of murder by a hitherto blameless bus driver, Lee Holbrook, who killed an eighteen year old student who rejected his sexual advances and who sealed her fate by threatening to report him to the authorities.

There is too a tendency to 'explain' aberrant behaviour in terms of the inability to form emotional attachments. Is this a matter of seeing a mode of behaviour and giving it a name? One of the latest is 'reactive attachment disorder', and how is *this* to be treated? Possibly by confronting and physically restraining children by the innovative Foster Cline method? Obviously some modern therapists are discovering that the old methods still work.

Understandably, some feel that any explanation is better than no explanation. But the problem is how to relate the theory to the practice. And here again we are confronted by the issue of incommensurability,. If we return for a 'moment to the question of brain damage: if-there is, for example, the equivalent of three cubic millimetres of frontal lobe damage, how can this be translated into degrees of culpability? And how is this different from two cubic millimetres or four cubic millimetres or whatever? How is the degree of damage to be related to the gravity of the crime and the consequent sentence? When one considers the terrible nature of some crimes, one wonders if the term 'evil' should be re-introduced to the vocabulary.

When no obvious physical damage can be found in suspects it is always a reasonable ploy to fall back on otherwise neurotic conditions. In the notorious Jill Dando murder it is as well to remind ourselves that Barry George was duly handed over to the experts who 'discovered' that he was suffering from a bizarre array of disorders. He was diagnosed as being psychopathic, paranoid, narcissistic, histrionic, somatistic and autistic. In short, he had a 'concurrent factitious disorder'. But none of this actually proves that he was guilty of murder.

And what of the situation where the accused is au fait with the routines and knows the psychiatric game? In 1997, Paul Beart, who had been a good student at school (nine '0' levels and four 'A' levels) dropped out of university, and began a new 'career' as a sexual sadist. He was convicted of a sexual attack on a friend of the family, but was released on licence after serving only three years of a five year sentence. He boasted to other inmates that he knew how to work the system, and fool the experts whose task was to assess him for early release. Within five months he tortured and killed a thirty-one year old hotel assistant, Deborah O'Sullivan, in Cornwall, a horrific crime for which he was sentenced to. life. At long last he was diagnosed as incurable, and – as always – the prison service, the probation service and the Home Office purported to have 'learned lessons'.

The search for physical factors which are thought to explain and even predict criminality goes back a long time. Some nineteenth century theorists such as the Italian psychiatrist, Cesare Lombroso seriously advanced the' hypothesis that hereditary criminals could be identified by certain well-defined physical characteristics. Yet this now discredited form of biological determinism has been given a new – and much more refined – lease of life by the intriguing science of molecular biology. But what can the study of DNA actually tell us about criminality as opposed to identifying the criminal?

We might glance briefly at the case of Stephen Mobley who was tried in Georgia in 1995 for shooting the manager of a restaurant. His lawyers offered a 'genetic appeal', arguing that in four generations the Mobley line was replete with unsavoury characters including one other murderer and an armed robber. But the prosecution reminded the jury that this was a very one-sided view, and made much of the fact that Mobley's father was a self-made millionaire – a fact that might well appeal to American juries but which might also hint at a little criminality too.. The faulty enzyme approach (borrowed from an earlier Dutch study) did not convince the court, and Mobley withdrew the plea.

As with the brain-damage defence, genetic dysfunction in some form or another is held by its advocates not so much as an explanation – certainly not as a sufficient cause – of crime, but something which may indicate a *predisposition*, especially to violence. As such, it could be regarded as mitigation, and therefore as a factor in determining degrees of blame and thus presumably forms of treatment or punishment. The debate continues. The neuroscientists are in disarray. Many insist that the evidence of a causal connection between the genes and crime just isn't there.

The still ongoing Nature-Nurture debate in the Behavioural Sciences may be wearing a little thin simply because there is a growing consensus that the human personality is not formed exclusively by one the other but is an amalgum of both. Indirectly, this controversy – as we have seen – is related to the age-old Free Will-Determinism controversy which has taken on a new life with the development of the science of genetics. This, as science writer Torsten Wiesel has pointed out, is most disturbing because it affects our sense of freedom and individuality. Can our personality – indeed, what we call our character including our mental abilities and propensities – be determined or destroyed by a segment of DNA?

Research into the possible relationship between genetics and crime is illuminating if only for the degree of controversy it has aroused. After all, no one has yet discovered a 'criminal gene'. There have been doubts about the research methodology and disputes about the validity of the findings themselves. Can behavioural traits and tendencies really be quantified in any meaningful way? Are environmental factors too many and varied to be clearly identified? And isn't the whole debate underlaid – as some claim- with complicating ideological (race, class, gender) presuppositions?

Genetic engineering of one kind or another has been going on for years. In certain of its recent forms such as cloning, one might well ask not so much whether or not it is ethically acceptable, as the more mundane question as to whether it is really necessary (Isn't one of the prevailing problems with science that just because it *can* be done, it actually *is* done?). Yet surely few would argue that if science was able to identify genes which seem to be responsible for certain inherited disabling diseases, genetic engineering would be both valid and desirable. So if it is the *cause* that really matters, could it actually be so reprehensible to manipulate the 'plumbing' in order to produce better individuals? This is, of course, *if* it can be done? Surely a more crime-free society is to be welcomed?

We can summarize, then, by saying that the entire issue is vitiated by three key assumptions:

i) that personality traits (involving behavioural performance) can be ranked in some qualitative way

ii) that crucial environmental factors can be identified

iii) that distinctive genetic factors can be quantified

These assumptions necessarily involve certain subjective assessments, and therefore still provoke considerable academic debate. Furthermore, the ethical factor precludes any really satisfactory experimentation on humans. So far, science has had to make do by extrapolating from animal studies as these yield,the only objective results. Needless to say, these may be seriously misleading as far as human behaviour in concerned.

If – or when – science is able to codify each individual's unique genome (involving some 80,000 genetic words), it may then be possible to organize a data base where every person's many characteristics can be checked and compared. Behaviour may then become predictable – and perhaps even modifiable. Indeed, at least one researcher, Harvey Lodish has suggested that there will be a time when an embryo's complete DNA will be analysed, and this information together with all possible environmental permutations will be fed into a supercomputer. The result will be a film in which the entire development of that individual will be depicted – possibly with ominous consequences for the embryo. This really will have heralded a 'Brave New World'.

It has become part of the current orthodoxy within certain sections of the academic – including criminological – fraternity that criminals (deviants?) are not entirely responsible for their actions. For whatever reason, physiological, psychological, social or in some sense broadly environmental, they have come to be seen as victims rather than criminals.. And because they are not irredeemably bad, they need treatment more than punishment. Yet note that between 1900 and 1965 (before capital punishment was abolished) the homicide rate in the UK averaged 350 per year. It has now more than doubled.

This is hardly overstating the case. All kinds of plausible – and not so plausible – reasons can be adduced by clever lawyers to either minimize of mitigate the guilt of their clients. (Interestingly at the lower levels of the legal system, for example where family lawyers are dealing with child protection, such mitigating arguments do not usually apply. It is immaterial whether the parents are alcoholics, drug dependent or just generally feckless, if the children are thought to be in danger, they are removed – an expedient which, effectively, 'punishes' the parents).

Some commentators have argued that to be 'morally deficient' is ipso facto to be ill. Maybe so. But although the vast majority of us are not overtly violent, and certainly do not kill, experience has shown that in certain situations (for example massacres/atrocities), it is clear that ordinary people are capable of the most horrendous acts (see Carlton, 1994). Perhaps therefore it can be cogently argued that murderers who kill gratuitously – without qualms – be removed from civilized society altogether.

It is surely time that we seriously questioned the current trend towards the medicalization of morality. But the tendency still persists. Do we really prefer to believe that criminals are mad rather than bad? And this without really convincing evidence. (Is it true that otherwise they wouldn't do what they do?). Can paedophilia really be simply attributed to disinhibition brought about by a decrease in serotonin levels? Or, as in the 1992 Weinstein case in the US, can metabolic imbalance traced to a tumour really justify a manslaughter charge for a man who strangled his wife and then threw her body out of a 12th floor apartment window? It is this kind of reasoning which can result in such bizarre verdicts as manslaughter instead of murder for Dan White in San Francisco in 1979 for the killing of the city mayor and one of his officials. Why? Well simply because White had apparently eaten too many cakes, and the excess sugar was deemed to have affected his brain chemistry and turned him into a killer. This all suggests a neuroscience in its most reductionist form.

Having said this, it is evident from our text that there are those who are seriously – and perhaps incurably – abnormal. There is clear evidence that some murderers who torture as well as kill are unalterably depraved, and certainly deserve the appellation – evil. What should be their fate? If we classify them as being deranged, for whatever reason, and that this should be taken into consideration when sentencing, it follows that the more heinous the crime the lighter the. sentence. A case could certainly be made that 'insanity' in such instances is not a basis for mitigation. And this regardless of the fact that the experts are still not clear as to just how we should define such a term, or even if such a definition is possible. Can we therefore justly find a place for ·such criminals in what we rather ambitiously refer to as 'civilised society'?

A similar problem is that of the murderer who has been re-socialized (= brain-washed?) into a new universe of meaning.' How else are we to regard the distorted values of the terrorist for example who kills the innocent in the perverted interests of a religious or quasi-religious ideology?

This text has taken a self-consciously moralistic stance. We can argue interminably about relativism and values, about the nuances of right and wrong, but it probably still remains true, as Kant insisted, that moral issues are not so much about intellectual uncertainty as an infirmity of the will. We are all tainted. What does the Confession say, 'There is no health in us'. Most of us are not as bad as we could be. But we are clearly not perfect. Maybe there are no such entities as 'good people', only people who sometimes do good things.

BIBLIOGRAPHY

ALBANESE, J. 1989, Organised Crime in America, Cincinnati: Anderson

ALEXANDER, R. 1987, The Biology of Moral Systems, New York: Aldine De Gruyter

ALLSOP, K, 1962, The Bootleggers, London: Hutchinson

BENN, S & PETERS, R. 1959, Social Principles of the Democratic State, London: Allen & Unwin

BEST, G, 1988, War and Society in Revolutionary Europe, Stroud: Sutton Publishing Co.

BIXLEY, W. 1957, The Guilty and the Innocent, London: Souvenir Press

BRUSSEL, J. 1968, Casebook of a Crime Psychiatrist, New York: Bernard Geis Associates

BURGER, R. 1995, Chavin and the Origins of Andean Civilisation, London: Thames & Hudson

BYLINSKY, G. 1973, New Clues to the Causes of Violence, Fortune Magazine, New York: Time Publications

CANTER, D. & YOUNGS, D. (Eds), 2008, Applications of Geographical Offender Profiling, Aldershot: Ashgate

CARLSON, N. 1987, Psychology: The Science of Behaviour, Boston, Mass: Allyn & Bacon

CARLTON, E. 1992, Occupation: The Policies and Practices of Military Conquerors, London: Routledge

CARLTON, E. 1995, Faces of Despotism, Aldershot: Scolar Press

CARLTON, E. 1995, Values and the Secial Sciences, London: Duckworth.

CARLTON, E. 1997, The State against the State, Aldershot: Scolar Press

CARLTON, E. 1998, Treason; Meaning and Motives, Aldershot: Ashgate

CARLTON, E. 2000, The Paranormal, Aldershot: Ashgate

CARLTON, E. 2001, Militarism: Rule without Law, Aldershot: Ashgate

CARRERE, E. 2000, The Adversary: a True Story of Murder and Deception. London: Bloomsbury

CARTER, R. 1999, Mapping the Mind, London: Orion

CATANZARO, R. transl. by Raymond Rosenthal, 1992, New York, The Free Press

CHECKLEY, H. 1976, Mask of Sanity, Saint Louis, Missouri: Mosby

CLARK, A. 1965, Barbarossa: The Russian German Conflict 1941–1945, London: Cassell

CLARKE, R. 1970, Crime in America, New York: Simon & Schuster

COHAN, A, 1975, Theories of Revolution, London: Nelson

COHEN, S. (revised 1980), Folk Devils and Moral Panics, London: Paladin

CONKLIN,J. 1977, The Crime Establishment, Englewood Clifts: Prentice Hall

CONQUEST, R. 1985, Inside Stalin's Secret Police, London: MacMillan

COOK, F. 1973, Mafia, New York: Coronet

COWEN P. 1979, An XYY Man, British Journal of Psychiatry 135

CULLEN, R. 1993, The Killer Department, London: Orion

DALLIN, A. 1981, German Rule in Russia 1941-45, London: MacMillan

DANK, M. 1978, The French against the French, London: Cassell

DARLEY, J., GLUCKSBERG, S & KINCHLAR, R. 1988, Psychology, (3rd Ed) Englewood Cliffs, New Jersey: Prentice-Hall

DAVIDOFF, L. 1980, Introduction to Psychology, (2nd Ed), New York: McGraw-Hill

DE HAAN, W. 1991 Abolitionism and Crime Control, in K. Stenson & D. Cowell (Eds), The Politics of Crime Control. London; Sage

ELLIS, L. & HOFFMAN, H. 1991, Crime in Biological, Social and Moral Contexts, New York: Praeger

EYSENCK, H. 1977, Crime and Personality, London: Paladin

FURNEAUX, R. 1967, They Died by the Gun, London: Mayflower-Dell

GAUTE, J. & ODELL, R. 1979, The Murderer's Who's Who, London: Pan Books

GIDDENS, A. 1991, Sociology, Oxford: Polity Press

GILBERT, M. 1989, Second World War, London: Weidenfeld & Nicholson

GRABER, G. 1980, History of the SS, London: MacMillan

HARE, R 1993, Without Conscience, New York: Warner Books

HASTINGS M. 1981, Das Reich London, Michael Joseph

HERZSTEIN, R. 1982, When Nazi Dreams Come True, London: Abacus

HESTER, S. & EGLIN, P. 1992, A Sociology of Crime, London: Routledge

HOHNE, H. 1969, Order of the Death's Head, London: Pan Books

HORNSBY, R & HOBBS, D. Gun Crime, Aldershot; Ashgate

HUGGETT, R & BERRY, P. 1956, Daughters of Cain, London: Allen & Unwin

JARY, D, & JARY, J. 1991, Dictionary of Sociology, London: Harper Collins

KATZ, L. 1973, Uncle Frank: The Biography of Frank Costello, New York: Drake

KEATING, W. & CARTER R, 1956, The Man who Rocked the Boat, London: Gollancz

KEFAUVER, E. 1951, Crime in America, New York; Doubleday

KELL Y, R 1986, Organised Crime: an International Perspective, Totowa, New Jersey: Doubleday

KERSHAW, A, 1955, Murder in France, London: Constable

KRAUSNICK, H. & BROSZAT, M. 1970, Anatomy of the SS State, London: Paladin

LAINES, M. & HENTY, S, 1998, Essential Criminology, Oxford: Westview Press

LARKIN, M. 1959, Seven Shares in a Gold Mine, London:.Gollancz

LEWIS, N. 1964, The Honoured Society, New York: Putnams

LEYTON, E. 1997, Men of Blood, Harmondsworth: Penguin

LINDSEY, P. 1958, The Mainspring of Murder, London: John Lang

LYOTARD, J. 1984 The Postmodern Condition: a Report on Knowledge, Minneapolis: University of Minnesota

MAAS, P. 1968, The Valachi Papers, New York: Putnams

MACLEAN, B. & MILOVANOVIC, D. 1991 Eds. New Directions in Critical Criminology, Vancouver: The collective Press

MAGUIRE, M., MORGAN, R. & REINER, R. 2007, The Oxford Handbook of Criminology, Oxford, Clarendon Press

MARSHALL, G. Ed., 1998, 2nd Edition, Oxford Dictionary of Sociology, Oxford: OUP

MARTIN, B. 1981, Abnormal Psychology: Clinical and Scientific Perspectives, New.york: Holt, Rinehart & Winston

MATTHEWS, R. 1989, The Power Brokers, Oxford: Facts on File

MEDNICK, S, & MOFFITT, Eds, 1986, The New Biocriminology, Cambridge: CUP

MOIR, A. & JESSEL, D. 1995, A Mind to Crime, London: Michael Joseph

MOQUIN, W. 1976, The American Way of Crime, New York: Praeger

MORRISON, W., 1995, Theoretical Criminology: from modernity to postmodernism London: Sage

MOUNTFIELD, D. 1979, The Partisans, London: Hamlyn

NASH, J. R. 1992, World Encyclopaedia of Organised Crime, London: Headline

ODELL, R. 1996 The International Murderer's Who's Who, London: Headline Publishing

OLWES, D., BLACK, J. & RADKE-YARROW, M. (Eds), 1986, Development of Antisocial and Prosocial Behaviour, New York: Academic Press

OVERY, R. 1984, Goering: The Iron Man, London: RKP

REID, W. 1978, The Psychopath, New York: Brunner/Mazel

REITLINGER, G. 1981, The SS – The-Alibi of a Nation, London: Arms & Armour Press

ROBINS, L. 1979. Sturdy childhood predictors of adult antisocial behaviour in J. Barnett, R. Rose, & G. Klerman (Eds) Stress and Mental Disorders, New York: Raven

ROBINS, L. & RUTTER, M. (Eds), 1990, Straight and Devious Pathways ftom Childhood to Adulthood, Cambridge, OUP

ROCK, P. (Ed.) 1988, A History of British Criminology, Oxford: OUP

ROWLAND, J. 1960, Poisoner in the Dock, London: Arco

SAGARIN, E. (Ed), 1980, Taboos in Criminology, Beverly Hills, LA: Sage

SERENY, G. 1991, Into that Darkness, London: Andre Deutsch Ltd.

SERENY, G. 2000, The German Trauma: Experiences and Reflections, Harmondsworth: Penguin

SHORT, M. 1986, Crime Inc, The Story of Organised Crime, London: Thames Methuen

SINGER, J. (Ed), 1971, The Control of Aggressions and Violence: Cognitive and Physiological Factors, New York: Academic Press

SMITH, E. 1994, The Sleep of Reason, London: Century

SONDERN, F. 1959, Brotherhood of Evil: The Mafia, New York: Farrar, Strauss & Condahy

SOROKIN, P, 1954, Fads and Foibles of Sociology, New York: Regnery

STEIN, M. 1995, Jung on Evil, London: Routledge

SUTHERLAND, E. 1949, Principles of Criminology, Chicago: Lippincott

TEREA, V. 1973, My Life in the Mafia, New York: Doubleday

TIERNEY, J. 1996, Criminology: Theory and Context, Hertfordshire: Wheatsheaf

TURKUS, B & FEDER, S. 1951, Murder Inc, The Story of the Syndicate, New York: Farrer, Strauss & Young

VOLD, G.B., BERNARD,J. & SNIPES, 1998, Theoretical Criminology, Oxford: OUP

WALKLATE, S. 1998, Understanding Criminology: Current Theoretical Debates, Buckingham, Open University Press

WEST, D.J. 1965, Murder followed by-Suicide, London: Heinemann

WEST, N. 1997, Faber Book of Treachery. London: Faber

WILKES, E, (Bd), 1999, Unsolved Crimes, London: Robinson

WILSON, J.Q. 1983, Thinking about Crime, New York: Basic Books

WILSON, S. & HERRSTEIN, P. 1985, Crime and Human Nature, New York: Simon & Schuster

WOLFGANG, M. 1966, Patterns of Criminal Homicide, Pennsylvania Science Editions, University of Pennsylvania Press

YOUNG, J. 1980, The Development of Criminology in Britain, British Journal of Criminology 28

YOUNG, J. 1988, Realist Criminology, London: Sage

ZAHN-WAXLER, C., CUMMINGS, M. & LANNOTTI, R. (Eds) 1986, Altruism and Aggression – Biological and social Origins, Cambridge: CUP

INDEX

Levy, A. 104
Leyton, E. 169
Liberation movements 42
Lohr General 147
Luciano, C. 125
Luftwaffe raids 100

'Mad Bomber Case' 59ff.,
Madero 135–6
Mafia 7, 16, 124ff.,
Mansfield, M. 12
Manson case 108–9
Markov, G. 138
Marshall, G. 9
Marxism 38–9, 40
Masada 110
Maslow, A. 176
Mau Mau 112
Maximillian 134
Mazatlan incident 69
McDonald, W. 57–8
McVeigh, T. 43
Menendez case 161
Merrett, D. 22
Merrifield case 79
Merton, R. 40
Mesopotamia 4
Metesky, G. 63ff.,
Mexico 134–8
Militancy 43–4
Mobley case 184
Mongols 145
Mont Fiona 103
Moral relativism 13–16, 17–18
Multinationals viii
Munchhausen's Syndrome 107
Munroe case 116–17

Murder 6, 22ff., 33ff., 55ff., 161ff.,
Murder Inc. 125ff.,

Napoleon 4, 181
Nazi hierarchy 85, 138, 145ff.,
Neilsen ('Black Panther') case 171
Nelson 'Baby Face' 39
Nichols, T. 43
Nilson case 96
NKVD/KGB 166
Norway 148
Nuremburg Trials 145–6, 151

Oklahoma City atrocity 43
Oliverotto 131–2
Opium trade 5
Oradour massacre 149–150
Ottomans 132–3

Paedophilia 28, 48
Palmer case 79
Parachute Regt. 55
Paraguay 133
Paramilitary Groups 4, 43
Parker, C. 29
Parkinson case 88
Patterson case 103–4
Peoples Temple case 109–10
Peru 145
Petiot case, 117–8, 166
Philby, K. 165–6
Philipinnes 144
Pilger, J. 141
Pincus, J. 182
Plato 16
Poland 147–8, 150ff.,
Police viii, 40, 41, 95, 130, 158, 179